Contents

Introduction — 2
Fiona Allan

This worked for me! — 3
Steve Pardoe, Former head of the Centres for Excellence in Maths project (CfEM)

What do we need to know about our learners? — 4
Jenny Stacey

A starter – the Swedish Number Game — 9
Tom McCormick

What I say when someone says "I can't do Maths" — 12
Natacha Shakil

Using double number lines to support proportional reasoning — 14
Byron Sheffield and Jane Barnett

Misunderstandings and misconceptions — 20
Fiona Allan

The use of the Socratic method to foster discussion — 25
Despoina Boli

Daily Maths — 29
Julia Smith

Language in the resit GCSE Maths classroom — 32
Jenny Stacey

Non-mathematical starters — 36
Despoina Boli

Engaging real-world investigations — 38
Martin Newton

Why I changed, "From Sage on the Stage to Guide on the Side" — 42
Joan Ashley

Mean, median, mode and range – a Standards Unit activity — 47
George Lane

Three sessions that worked for me — 50
Andrew Davies

Creating GCSE Maths revision cards — 55
Bernadette Evans

This book was compiled and edited by Fiona Allan, who is very grateful to the authors for writing their chapters.

Links to websites mentioned in the book can be found at **www.thisworkedforme.uk**

Introduction

During the last twenty years, I have worked on many different national projects with teachers of students resitting GCSE Maths. For example, I was one of the team leading the Maths Enhancement Programme which upskilled more than 2,000 FE teachers of other subjects to enable them to teach students resitting GCSE Maths. In many of the other national projects, we tested activities or approaches in a quest to find out what would help more students achieve a C or a 4/5.

Over the years, I have met many teachers who have told me about one or more activities or approaches that they feel have really worked for them and for their students. So, early last year, I started to ask FE teachers if they would be willing to write a chapter for this book or if they knew someone who might be willing to share their story.

This book is the result. It has been written by teachers who have thought deeply about what was happening in their resit GCSE Maths classroom. Some of them have used ideas and activities from national research projects such as The Standards Unit's *Improving learning in mathematics*, while others have developed their own ideas. Every chapter is written by someone who can say "This worked for me!"

Fiona Allan

This worked for me!

According to one of the book's authors, "... teaching learners who are resitting GCSE maths is a challenging task.". Many teachers would say this is an understatement! Generally, 16- to 19-year-olds in FE colleges and elsewhere arrive with profoundly negative experiences of learning maths, characterised by failure and anxiety, and are in need of a fresh approach and a shot of self-belief if they are to progress. To this end, *This worked for me!* provides a really valuable resource.

In the book, different teachers share their experiences of what they've found works – some focusing on specific activities, while others talk about more general approaches and teaching strategies. Many are self-created, while others draw on published resources. What they have in common is that they are tried and tested with FE learners – including adults and functional skills students, as well as 16-19 GCSE learners.

Each chapter provides an individual teacher perspective, but a common theme is learner-centredness, through engagement, thinking and understanding. Some authors highlight discussion and questioning techniques to achieve this, while others utilise visual models and contextualisation. It isn't all about "maths" though – several authors provide a welcome focus on the "affective domain" – addressing the anxiety and fixed mindsets that many learners present, and sharing ways of developing positive relationships by respecting and valuing individual learners' opinions, interests and preferred ways of learning. There's also a really useful chapter on maths language – an important topic that's often overlooked!

Chapters are short and easily accessible to busy teachers who would like to use, adapt or build-on the approaches. They may be used by individual teachers seeking ideas or inspiration, but could also be adopted by groups of teachers wanting to collaborate, and perhaps used as a basis for action research.

In short, *This worked for me!* is a welcome sharing of successful approaches - not only for FE teachers, but for all maths teachers who are struggling with low-achieving and disengaged maths learners.

Steve Pardoe
Former head of the Centres for Excellence in Maths project (CfEM)

What do we need to know about our learners?

Jenny Stacey

Jenny Stacey taught maths in an East Midlands FE college from 2004 until 2022. She has taught Key Skills, Basic Skills, ESOL maths, Functional Skills, and GCSE to adults and 16- to 18-year-olds, including ESOL/EAL students. Currently she is employed as an Associate Lecturer at Sheffield Hallam University.

New learners arrive in our GCSE resit mathematics classroom. They are taking GCSE Maths; so, either they have not achieved the magic "grade 4 or better" so far in their GCSE mathematics examinations, or for some reason they have never sat a GCSE Maths examination.

The learners in the first group can arrive with burdens of fear or anxiety about mathematics, maths examinations, or examinations generally. They may also have low confidence either about the maths, or about themselves, in the form of low self-esteem, because so far, they have "failed". Those in the second group may have newly arrived in the UK, or have sat their exams at schools in a different country, or have abandoned school at some point before the exams, but they may still have some or all of the feelings of the first group. Technically, of course, those in the latter category are not resit students, if they have never taken the exam before, but all these people are in our classes, regardless of age, gender, ethnicity, or what first language they speak.

What works for me when dealing with these highly diverse, but very exciting, groups of learners is to find out more about them than can be gleaned from any initial or diagnostic assessments and past exam results. I am not saying that these assessments or exam results will not be useful - they will, especially when it comes to the decisions on target setting, and whether they should be sitting Foundation or Higher tier papers, but initial assessments and diagnostic assessments do not give us a full picture of who these learners are, and what issues they may have.

I believe that if we know what challenges these learners face, we can better prepare them for a successful outcome in terms of exam results.

How do I find out about these learners?

I use a short questionnaire to find out more about them. The questionnaire I am going to share with you, has been developed over many years of delivery of GCSE Maths to FE learners of all ages (16 to 18 years and those in adults' classes). It has been developed and refined over the years and draws on many other questionnaires that include maths anxiety or self-efficacy (confidence in one's ability). The latest version has emerged from what participants in my doctoral research found to be most important or critical. It can be handed out on paper or completed as an online form.

The use of a questionnaire is both practical and psychological. Not only will you find out if the learners' perceptions match their abilities, which they may not, but the sharing of those perceptions can be cathartic for learners, and again, there is a lot of research to support this. It is worth saying at the start that responses are confidential unless they agree or choose otherwise.

I usually run the questionnaire around the third week of the first term, as that gives learners time to settle in, and reduces the impact of "new class, new classmates, new teacher, new room, new course, new routine …". It can also improve relationships in the classroom, as learners can see that you are interested in them as individuals, rather than viewing the whole class as a homogenous mass.

Feel free to use, adapt or refine the questionnaire for your students!

What do we need to know about our learners?

The maths and exams confidence survey (MECS)

Name ....

Colour preference .... *(See top of page 7 for explanation)*

Date ....

Think about the situation described and rate how confident you would feel about your ability in each case. Tick the box, and write in the score:

Task	Very confident 1	Quite confident 2	Don't know 3	I don't think I can do this 4	I can't do this 5
Using a times table grid to find out what 7 × 9 is					
Drawing graphs and charts					
Working out 12% of £42					
Finding two thirds of £42					
Working out word problems, such as "If it takes 3 people 5 days to fit a kitchen, how long would it take 2 people?"					
Solving an algebraic equation, such as "If $3x - 2 = 7$, what is the value of x?"					
Asking a question in a maths class about something you have not understood					

©2024 ATM

Think about the following situations. How anxious you would feel in each case?

Tick and write each score:

Task	No anxiety 1	Some anxiety 2	Moderate anxiety 3	Quite a bit of anxiety 4	High anxiety 5
Thinking about an upcoming maths test one day before					
Taking the final maths exams at the end of your course					
Taking other exams that are NOT maths					

What is your **total** score? Write it here: .... [Minimum 10; maximum 50]

Do you have any comments about any of the above? If so, please write them below or overleaf.

....

....

....

....

Justification for each part of the questionnaire

Name

We need to know the person's name, so we can identify them in class and cater to their needs, whether those are about the maths, or the exams, or both. We can also identify which aspects of the maths are considered "easy" by individuals, so that we can boost their confidence with these, and which are not, and so need work.

Also, I find that it is good to run the questionnaire again around April, to see how the learners' perceptions have altered. These alterations can be for better or for worse, the importance of which will be addressed shortly.

Note that I have *not* included age, gender, ethnicity or first language (whether it is English or not). This is because my research has shown that stereotypical assumptions about FE learners can be inappropriate and unhelpful!

Colour preference

I have a set of coloured overlays and reading panes that I circulate around the class in weeks 1 or 2, to identify those who have a colour preference for paper and other resources. This is a great ice breaker with a purpose! Some of your learners may be very happy with black writing on white paper, but others may find it very tiring, and really benefit from a coloured overlay that they can put over the worksheet or the computer screen, to help prevent tiredness and "the letters and numbers moving about all over the place", as one of my learners said.

The preference for a coloured overlay, especially if it is a strong colour, may be a marker for those with undiagnosed dyslexia or other issues. For instance, some of my learners have needed dark yellow, dark blue or dark green.

Coloured overlays or reading panes are available from special needs support, online, or from many opticians.

Date

The date learners complete the questionnaire is useful here, as, if time and management permit, you will hopefully be able to run the questionnaire again around April to see how learners are getting on. Is that student still as concerned about algebra, or word problems, or have their perceptions improved?

Most importantly, has anyone's self-efficacy declined, and/or anxiety levels risen in the run up to the exams? This can indicate exam anxiety, and these students may benefit from exam techniques, such as calming their breathing to reduce the panic or perhaps a smaller exam room, rather than the exam hall, or a short break part way through. Subsequent courses may depend on the exam results, and this pressure can raise stress levels, which can be counterproductive for some learners. It is worth helping students with exam techniques if it helps them to make progress.

If learners could benefit from more help than you can offer in the classroom, approach your organisation for access to others who can help, or visit the Maths Anxiety Trust website[1], and the government web page on coping with exam pressure[2].

Self-efficacy

The self-efficacy section is mostly about aspects of the course content that have emerged from my research and experience as being most crucial for learners.

The times table statement could be seen as an easy lead in, but some people do not find reading tables easy. Drawing charts and graphs drew a real "love it or hate it" split for my research participants. Percentages and fractions: some seem to like one and some the other, and some neither.

Word problems emerged as an area of difficulty which was seen by my participants as equally challenging as algebra. This was a surprise, and I think shows that we need to spend more time encouraging learners, perhaps through paired work, to engage with these types of questions. Our students need to have the confidence to try these questions, and if their chosen strategy does not look correct, to try another one, rather than render their answer unreadable, or leave the question blank.

On the subject of algebra, some seem to get it, some do not. I love it myself, and there are usually a few students in the room who agree with me. I use matching activities to start students off with algebra, but time may be better spent improving other skills for Foundation learners. Higher tier students should be encouraged to at least attempt questions. One of my learners had a bag printed for me at the end of the academic year; it had a big smiley face and on it was written "Do algebra, Be happy". I love that bag.

Finally, asking a question in class about something that you have not understood. I was astonished at the responses to this statement in my research, because some of those learners who got the best grades, as well as others, felt that they could not do this, thus it was not grade specific. As a teacher, if I know who will not be able to ask a question in class, I can quietly check that those learners are OK when I set the class off on work, and then go round the room.

Anxiety

The anxiety section concentrates on timed testing. This can be very stressful for many of our learners, and tests can be just as stressful as final exams. If learners are very stressed about tests, they may not even turn up on the test day, so it might be better to employ subterfuge: "There may be a test at some point in the next week or two" will alert those that want to revise that the time has come, but hopefully not drive some students away!

The question about maths exams is perhaps obvious, but the interesting bit is other exams: do your students feel as anxious about other exams as about maths? If so, this may indicate general exam anxiety, if not, then it is specifically maths exams that are causing an issue. This will affect the kind of support that will need to be offered to maximise the chances of success, as discussed above.

Total score

At the end learners can add up their score themselves, or you can do it for them. This total will give you an overview, but I find that it is the individual components of the questionnaire that are of most interest. The overall scores will give you a comparison with the second questionnaire and might help if you need to argue for additional support, specific resources, or smaller classes.

Additional comments

In FE, there are often differences in teaching and learning practice that students will not have experienced at school, and it can be these differences that can help learners to re-engage with subjects where they may previously have struggled.

Some people will leave the additional comments section blank, but others will write and write and write. They may share their feelings about school, fellow students, or their experiences of maths classes. The maths and exams confidence survey will fit onto an A4 sheet, or two sides of an A5, so learners will have space to write if they want to. This can be a very cathartic process for learners.

In class or not?

I have done this both ways with paper-based questionnaires, so it is up to you, but as you are collecting these in, then in class with some groups will be essential.

When I did the questionnaires with one class, I told the group that their responses would be confidential, just between them and me to help inform my teaching and support, but on completion the room erupted into a 10-minute conversation and debate whilst learners compared scores and answers. This really worked with this group, as everyone realised that even those who did not seem to be struggling with the maths, or who looked really confident in class, all had their issues, weak spots, and fears around timed testing. In short, they loved it!

In other classes, learners have mostly completed these online, using phones or laptops, and the discussion and debate have been limited to close friends and whispered comparisons. In this case, in the following lesson I initiated a discussion about the similarity of their responses, and highlighted subject areas where more work could be helpful.

Finally

This approach does not suit all learners, and it will not suit all teachers either, but I hope that you will try it and see if it improves both learners' outcomes, and relationships with and between your FE learners. It has certainly worked for me!

---

1 – *https://mathsanxietytrust.com/*

2 – *https://www.gov.uk/government/publications/coping-with-exam-pressure-a-guide-for-students/coping-with-exam-pressure-a-guide-for-students*

A starter – the Swedish Number Game

Tom McCormick

For almost a decade, Tom has taught students resitting GCSE Maths in various colleges across the UK, in roles such as Lecturer, Program Lead, and Curriculum Lead.

What works for me, is a game I saw whilst in Sweden and regularly use as a starter activity.

Like many activities, I decided to try this game spontaneously when I saw the expressions on students' faces and realised that I needed to do something to bring some energy into the room. One of the great things about this game is it requires zero prep or resources, so it really can be used with no pre-planning.

I have had discussions with various peers and colleagues about the benefits of using games in the resit classroom. Whilst some people might be concerned that older students may consider them childish, I believe that the age group we typically teach can still be energised by beginning with a competitive, low-stakes game. These can also provide the opportunity for some subtle assessment for learning at the start of a session, again with low stakes.

The game works as follows

Students draw two rows of three boxes. Each box should be big enough to hold a single digit. These will ultimately make a pair of three-digit numbers.

Two rows of three boxes (Hundreds, tens and ones)

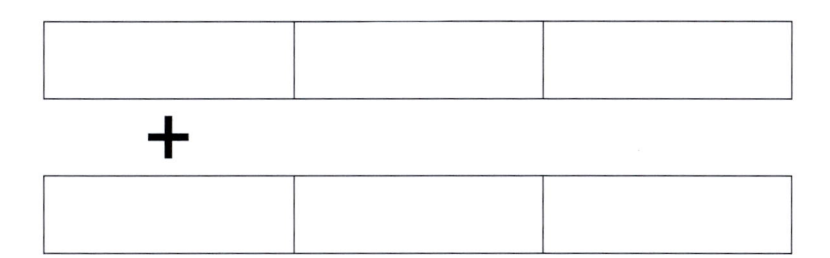

\+

Their goal is to add the two rows together in order to achieve the highest possible sum. The largest answer wins, and some may be surprised at how competitive the students get over quite a simple game. I make a point of saying to the students that they don't need to draw carefully or use a ruler. This is because, from my experience, many learners spend unnecessary time and effort drawing perfectly ruled tables when there is no need.

You then call out a single-digit number, and the learners must put it in one of the boxes. Once a number is placed, it cannot be moved. Therefore, students need to carefully consider where they place numbers and what numbers could potentially come after.

I use a random number generator from Google on the main board to ensure fairness. This way, students can see that I haven't intentionally selected a specific number to ruin their chances. But if you prefer, you could call out random numbers instead.

A starter – the Swedish Number Game

The random number generator shows a 9. Students place 9 in one of the six boxes.

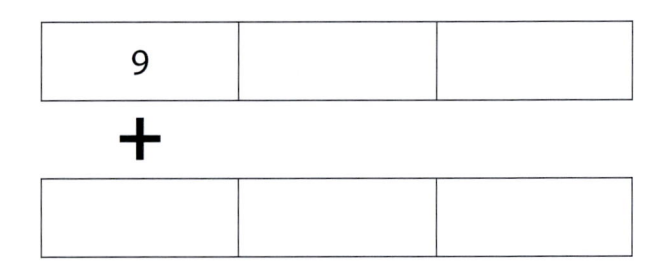

You repeat the process until all six boxes are full and students have both three-digit numbers. You'll notice that I have modified the range on the number generator to include numbers from 0 to 9. However, occasionally introducing a 10 into the game can lead to confusion among students as they try to determine how it fits within the table. Interestingly, this confusion often prompts them to think more deeply about place value than the rest of the game. Therefore, I highly recommend incorporating this intentional mistake occasionally.

Students fill the boxes one by one until complete. Numbers in boxes cannot be changed once placed.

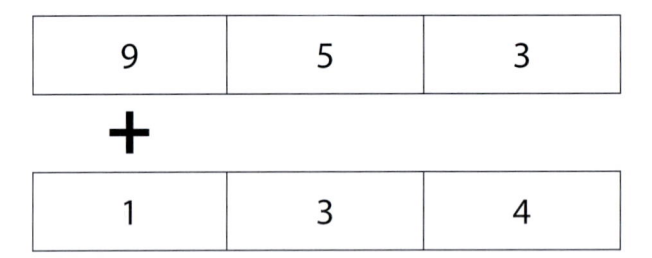

Students then add those two rows together (without a calculator), so in the above example, their answer would be 1087. The largest correct number wins. I always check which two numbers they obtained, as this can lead to two interesting conversations, namely "Is that the best possible outcome with those six numbers?" and "I got the same answer but from different numbers, how does that work?"

One of my colleagues uses ten sided dice, and groups of students roll the die to generate the numbers instead of leading the task from the front. The students seem to like the tactile nature of the die.

Links to curriculum

People who are new to the resit scene are often surprised by the extent to which post-16 learners may lack a genuine understanding of number systems and place value. Without full mastery of this, they will always be less fluent in higher-level topics. This game challenges numerical logic, where students need to understand that the first numbers are the most significant, while the units are the least significant. This concept of place value is extended further in the scenario mentioned above, where different numbers yield the same correct answer. Similarly, when working with students resitting GCSE, we may mistakenly assume that students who achieved certain grades in the past are already proficient in addition and subtraction without a calculator. By playing this game early in the year, I have been able to identify some students who still need support in this area and provide them with the necessary assistance. As I'll cover with my adaptations, I frequently adjust this game in order to test other non-calculator skills. It is important to remember the non-calculator paper makes up an often undervalued third of marks in GCSE Maths (or half of the WJEC marks).

At the end, I always ask a simple question: "What was the best possible answer using those six numbers?". This is a not uncommon question in GCSE exams where students are asked to arrange a set of digits to create the largest possible number.

Adaptations

As the year progresses, I use slightly different versions of this now-familiar game to either extend or use slightly different skills. I have provided a few examples below, but I am sure there are many more that people will come up with.

The smallest answer wins: This doesn't change much of the game, but it does just test students' understanding that this numerical logic works in both directions. Also, this can be a good test of who has been listening to the instructions, which is another reason I use this example.

Subtraction: This is a simple change, but it significantly increases the level of numerical logic required. Many learners often start by creating the two largest numbers without realising that they should be subtracting the smallest number possible.

Multiplication: I only tend to do this with two 2-digit numbers, purely for time reasons. This a good way of testing another important non-calculator skill.

Decimals: Essentially putting a decimal point into the original grid and then playing as normal. The main reason I like using this example later in the year is that it perfectly demonstrates that adding decimals is no different from adding integers, as long as you don't lose sight of the place value.

Layout for decimals version

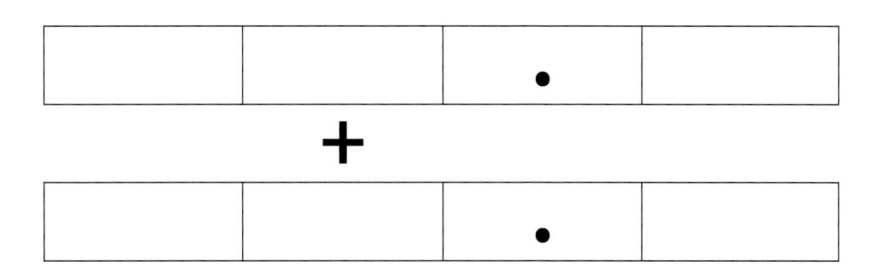

		•	

+

		•	

Estimation: The same game but asking students to use estimation in working out their answers. This is useful because I find that although students tend to understand the concept of estimation easily, they often need more repetition when it comes to being required to round to one significant figure.

Specify odd/even answers only: This again tests another element of students' numerical logic and number systems. GCSE exam questions also like to test this somewhere across the papers, so this offers a nice assessment for learning point to ensure learners are proficient at this.

I'm certain that you will think of many different versions or changes you could use for your own classes. After all, the best advice I've ever received about teaching in further education is to share as many resources as possible. However, it is important to remember you can customise them to fit your own style. Similarly, it is beneficial to observe other teachers and learn from them, but never attempt to simply replicate their teaching methods. Instead, teach in a way that makes you feel comfortable.

What I say when someone says "I can't do Maths"

Natacha Shakil

Natacha left school with no qualifications and, after having four children, decided to go to college and become a maths teacher. Her passion has always been to support those that struggle the most and, when they achieve, there are not many other things that top that feeling.

Why is it in the UK, we find it socially acceptable to say, "I can't do maths" or "My parents couldn't do maths and they were fine". When our students say this about their parents, we have to ask were they fine or did they really need to be able to do maths? A friend is dyslexic and although undiagnosed is probably on the autistic spectrum. He has always struggled with education and the formality of the classroom. However, he always had an interest in fixing things and preferred hands-on activities, and he became a multi-skilled maintenance man. If you ask him, he can't do maths, but he can look at a room and tell you how many tins of paint you need, or how many lengths of skirting board are required, because he has calculated this in his head. So he can do maths, just not in the traditional setting of a school or college.

Even as maths teachers, we struggle to explain the usefulness of certain topics in real life. How many times have we used quadratic equations in daily life? But is the usefulness of maths and application of maths knowledge the sole reason for studying maths? What if by completing a quadratic equation, we are actually demonstrating our problem solving skills, resilience, attention to detail and application of knowledge? Isn't this what we should be explaining to our learners?

In post-16 resit Maths classes, our learners have supposedly "failed" at school. In most cases, they achieved a grade but they haven't gained a grade 4 or above yet. So we need to consider the language we use when working with these learners and we are challenged with changing their mindset.

Learners come to us with the knowledge they haven't "passed" GCSE Maths, but maybe they were in a lower set at school, where they were not expected to reach a grade 4; maybe they didn't have a teacher with a qualification in maths; maybe they didn't have sufficient support at home; maybe they are a young carer - the possibilities are endless. What we do know is that they need someone to believe in them, someone to help them change from a fixed mindset to a growth mindset, someone to inspire and motivate them. Their emotions, attitudes, motivations and values all prevent them from committing and trying their best, because rather than look stupid, they will be a little cheeky, need lots of toilet breaks, go on their phone, chat to their friends etc.

I believe that their feelings need to be recognised, acknowledged and validated in order to move forward. Indeed, most of these learners have developed some level of maths anxiety and in their minds, maths is associated with failure. Thinking of Maslow's hierarchy of needs, physiological, safety and belonging, we need to create a safe encouraging learning environment in which they can flourish. Sue Johnston-Wilder, Associate Professor (Teaching Focussed) at Warwick University and who works with the Maths Anxiety Trust, uses the metaphor of a car and a handbrake to describe the impact of maths anxiety on a learner, suggesting that we are trying to push a car with the handbrake on. Until that emotional handbrake is released, learners are unlikely to make progress in maths.

One of my most impactful resources has been my introductory lessons at the beginning of the year, which consist of building relationships, developing a growth mindset, understanding the growth zone and setting out their expectations and my expectations for the year. I continue to refer to these throughout the year.

Through action research I have developed a method of combatting this emotional handbrake by asking my learners to write on a post it/sticky note what they dislike about maths and on another one positive thing about maths.

I find that the learners need lots of coaching to record one positive thing, but this is an extremely important part of the process. In contrast, they will record plenty of dislikes and I reassure them that that is OK.

The typical negative answers will be:

- I had a non-maths teacher/supply teachers teaching my maths class;
- I don't like exams; or
- I don't like algebra, fractions, decimals etc.

The positives usually include statements like:

- I had one good teacher who explained it well; or
- I like/liked a particular topic.

I collect the responses in two groups - positives and negatives, and then group them into themes such as teachers, or topics. Then I try to balance the positives and the negatives against each other, for example, I had a good teacher, against I had a bad teacher. It's important to frame the mindset around these situations when you're discussing the statements, e.g. "My teachers hated me" (fixed mindset) contrasting to "my teacher in year 10 didn't like me" (growth mindset).

I emphasise that poor experiences don't have to define your whole life, they are specific to a timeframe. Just because that teacher disliked you, doesn't mean I will dislike you; you respect me and I will respect you. When dealing with dislike of particular topics, I tell the learners that it's not all about the topic, it's about the wider skills set which is being developed as they study that topic.

If there are any negatives still to be dealt with, I then reassure them, saying that I intend to support them and will try different things to see if it helps, such as active learning or maths models. I also believe that it is important to let them know I am not perfect. I often use the example that I make mistakes on the board and it's OK for them to tell me if they spot a mistake. I explain that sometimes I might try a different approach or activity and if it doesn't go to plan, we have to work together to move forward. I believe that the learners have to make a commitment to trying their best during their resit year.

A further benefit of this activity is they see other students in the class have had similar experiences to them and they are not alone. Doing this activity seems to develop a sense of community within the class. This activity has worked well across all vocational areas, including construction, sports, hair and beauty etc.

I had the privilege of writing three lessons for the Centre for Excellence in Maths (CfEM) scheme of learning. Two of these lessons encompassed these strategies and theories that support learners to overcome anxieties and barriers. These lessons have brought together FE specific action research from across the country. Do have a look at the Education and Training Foundations' *GCSE maths resits: Classroom resources*[1] lessons 1 and 2 where you will find lesson plans and PowerPoints.

I believe that this approach has had the greatest impact on my teaching.

---

[1] – https://www.et-foundation.co.uk/professional-development/maths-and-english/cfem/cfem-resources-and-evidence/teaching-for-mastery-classroom-resources/gcse-maths-re-sits-classroom-resources/

Using double number lines to support proportional reasoning

Byron Sheffield and Jane Barnett

Byron has been teaching for 34 years across the secondary and sixth form sectors. He has recently been working at Leyton Sixth Form College in London and was a centre lead for the Centres for Excellence in Mathematics project, which worked to improve the progress of level 2 Maths students in FE.

Jane has been a classroom maths teacher for over 20 years and is still learning how to do it. She works at Leyton Sixth Form College in Northeast London and is passionate about the way getting the right grade in GCSE Maths can change your life.

Have you ever had a student come out of an exam and complain that you never taught them anything about watermelons, or how to convert cubic metres to seconds?

You know, as a maths teacher, that this question definitely wasn't really about watermelons, and that there definitely was some information there about a rate connecting volume to time, but the student hasn't picked out that information from a wordy question. They need a tool that helps give them some structure to the information in a question that has been set in an unfamiliar context. The tool needs to represent the information more clearly, highlight what they need to work out, and then give them a framework to use their creativity to find a solution.

Through our research, we've learned that it's not enough just to show students a diagram or model, you need to actively teach them to use it. That takes time, so you want to choose a diagram that is versatile to get the most re-use from it. A double number line is such a diagram. A double number line is a simple thinking tool inspired by the work of the Realistic Maths Education project[1] and of Geoff Wake[2] at the University of Nottingham and is particularly helpful for proportional reasoning. It's easy to draw and shows two parallel axes, one for each connected variable. The axes do not have to be drawn to scale or fully labelled but they do give an indication of whether the answer will be larger or smaller. Huge amounts of GCSE Maths are connected to proportional reasoning (especially at Foundation tier) so this is a great place to focus your efforts.

Scan the QR code to read our first research paper where we experimented with teaching proportion using double number lines.

Here are a few topics where you can use double number lines:

- Direct proportion
- Best value
- Recipe questions
- Exchange rates
- Conversions
- Scale drawings and similar shapes
- Speed, distance and time
- Percentages

Let's see how we can use a double number line for a past exam question on speed:
Emily drives 186 miles in 3 hours.
What is her average speed?

The examiner's report says:
*"There were a lot of distance, speed, time triangles, but not all were correct and those that were written in the correct orientation were not always used correctly. ... **The most common error seen was to multiply the figures.**"*

Start by setting up a double number line with your two variables. I've labelled the zero line here because one way to know this is direct proportion is that if the journey takes 0 time, you don't go anywhere (0 miles) – but with practice you don't really need to label the zero line.

```
0
|─────────────────────────────────▶ distance (miles)

|─────────────────────────────────▶ time (hours)
0
```

Add in the information that we have

```
                              186
|─────────────────────────────┼───▶ distance (miles)

|─────────────────────────────┼───▶ time (hours)
                               3
```

Speed is measured in miles per hour, that is how far you would go in one hour, so let's add that on to the diagram.

```
            ?                 186
|───────────┼─────────────────┼───▶ distance (miles)

|───────────┼─────────────────┼───▶ time (hours)
            1                  3
```

You could include more divisions, perhaps the distance in 2 hours, and this can be helpful at first when you are exploring the tool in a more open-ended way, but it can get very busy when there's a lot of information on the diagram.

Now we need to think about how we can move from one number to another **using only multiplying or dividing**. There are two ways to do this, working between the lines or working along the lines.

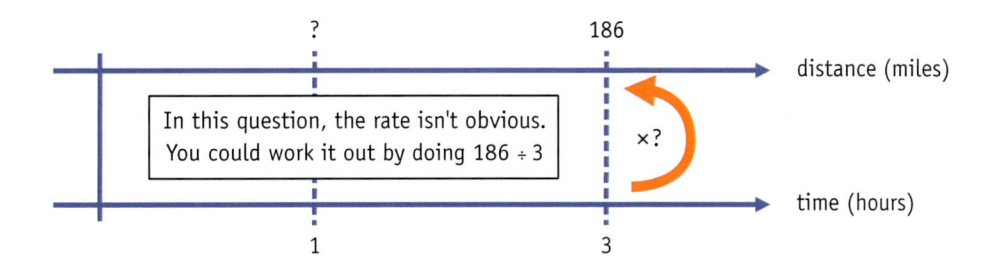

```
            ?                 186
|───────────┼─────────────────┼───▶ distance (miles)
        ┌──────────────────┐    ⤴
        │ In this question, the rate isn't obvious. │  ×?
        │ You could work it out by doing 186 ÷ 3    │
        └──────────────────┘
|───────────┼─────────────────┼───▶ time (hours)
            1                  3
```

For this question it's easier to see what's happening working along the lines. The scale factor is 3, and because the things we are measuring are proportional we divide by 3 along both lines.

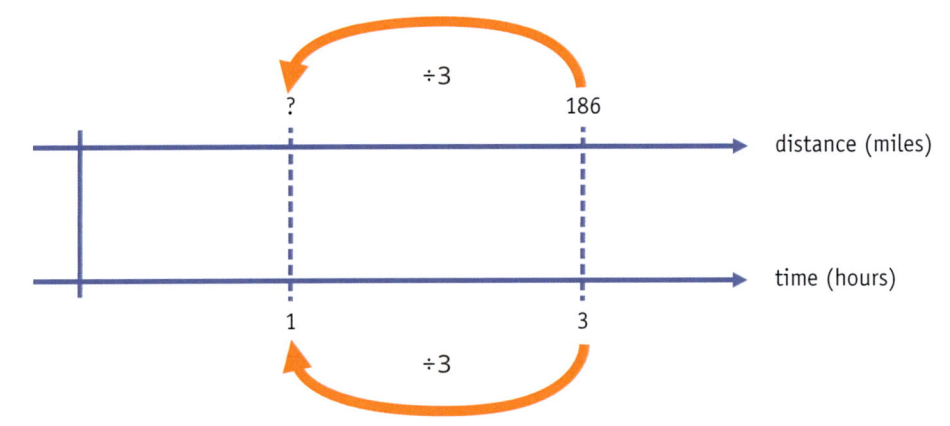

One area of the curriculum we were really interested in using double number lines was with percentages. This is because data from Pearson, looking at what topics showed the widest gap between grade 3 and grade 4 students in exams, had percentages right at the top. We linked this to our own experience of teaching this to our students where we knew they felt like they were being taught a slightly different method for each type of percentage question. The reason many of our students are retaking is because they can't remember or correctly apply lots of seemingly random methods. We feel that the way that double number lines show relationships between percentages and amounts means they can be used in the same way to solve any type of percentage question.

Scan the QR code to read about our research teaching percentages to mixed ability classes using double number lines.

Let's look at some examples to illustrate this:

a) Find 30% of £85

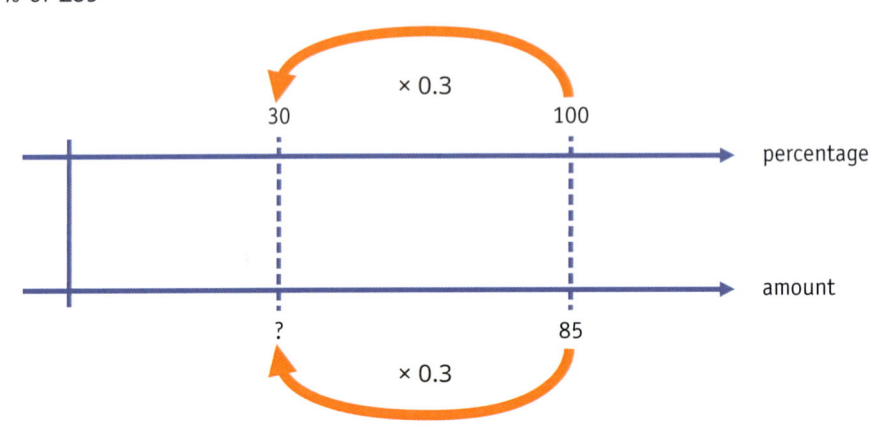

Having labelled the information on the diagram, students can now choose a method they are comfortable with to find the final amount. This could be dividing 100% down to an intermediary number like 1% or 10% and then multiplying up to 30%. As students become more confident, we encourage them to work out and use the direct multiplier as often as possible using a calculator, in this case 100 × 0.3 = 30, so 85 × 0.3 = £25.50

b) Write 30 out of 85 as a percentage

Once we have set up diagram with the information, we are now repeating the process of finding a missing number using multipliers or dividers. One approach is shown here.

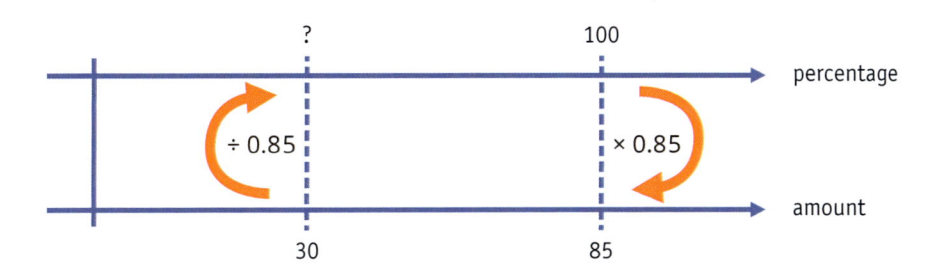

Using double number line to support proportional reasoning

```
                    ?              100
                    ┊               ┊
        ━━━━━━━━━━━━┿━━━━━━━━━━━━━━━┿━━━━━━━▶ percentage
                 ↷  ┊               ┊  ↶
                ÷ 0.85             × 0.85
        ━━━━━━━━━━━━┿━━━━━━━━━━━━━━━┿━━━━━━━▶ amount
                    ┊               ┊
                    30              85
```

c) A shirt is 15% off in a sale. It now costs £30. What did it cost originally?

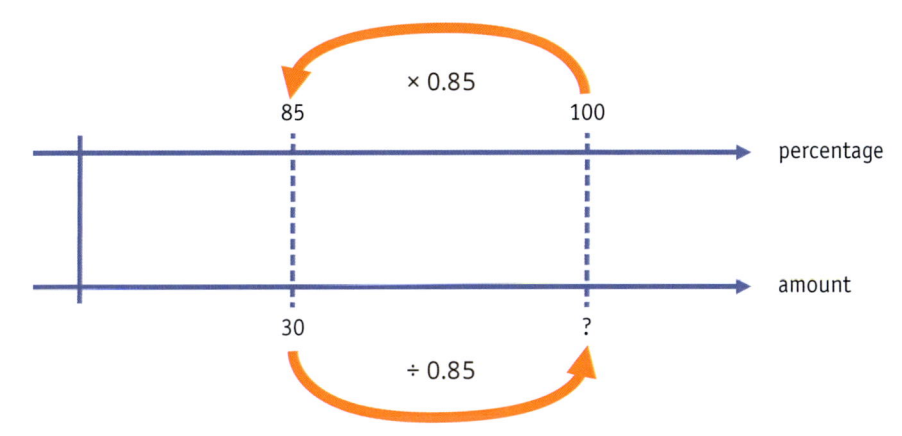

```
                        × 0.85
                    ↶━━━━━━━━━━↷
                    85         100
                    ┊           ┊
        ━━━━━━━━━━━━┿━━━━━━━━━━━┿━━━━━━━▶ percentage
                    ┊           ┊
                    ┊           ┊
        ━━━━━━━━━━━━┿━━━━━━━━━━━┿━━━━━━━▶ amount
                    ┊           ┊
                    30          ?
                    ↳━━━━━━━━━━↰
                        ÷ 0.85
```

This is the type of question that many students misread but the focus on what the original amount is and labelling the diagram make this far more accessible with a double number line. Our research showed that students who had their own good methods for the first two examples often struggled with this type of question and were willing to use this diagram and more often than not got the question right.

So now you've seen how to use a double number line, let's talk about how you teach people to use it.

1. **Make sure you know how to use it** in the context you plan to use it in. If possible, get a group of colleagues to try doing the questions you want students to do using double number lines – it's likely you won't all solve the problem the same way and it's helpful if you've seen some valid alternatives before you're live in the classroom.

2. **Model how to do an example** using a double number line in class. An example/problem pair is a good idea. We have made a whole set of power points and videos with slick animations but if we are honest there is a lot of value in showing how you can draw one by hand as a quick sketch – this is a thinking tool.

3. **Check** they can set up the diagram. Mini whiteboards are good for this.

4. **The original amount being 100%** is a key point in percentage work that is often missed by students, but is central to putting the information on the diagram.

5. **Emphasise** the importance of **just multiplying and dividing** – consider showing an example where someone has just subtracted from both numbers instead of dividing and ask students to explain to you what the problem is.

6. **Scaffold at first, but then withdraw it.** A matching activity where they match the diagram to the question then finish the question can work, or just a worksheet where there are diagrams to complete for the first section and then a second section where they are instructed to draw their own.

7. **Insist that they practise** drawing the diagram for every question for the duration of the lesson where you teach it. After that, they may or may not use it independently, but **remind them about this as a strategy if they are stuck**, especially towards exam time as they begin to work through past papers.

8. **Have some extension questions.** Students who have their own methods may not want to use the diagram. Take a look at their own method and see if they can extend it/adapt it to harder, non-standard questions, or for proof. They might then value learning another strategy that they can use when they need it. **When students are describing their methods to you (or to the class) try to model it on a double number line** at the same time.

9. **Refresh** it in a recall starter, especially if you're going to use it again in a new context.

10. **Prompt** students to use the approach in internal assessments by adding a blank double number line template for them with relevant questions.

We have used our classroom trials to work out how best to implement and use double number lines with our students and we have seen the positive impact this has had on both their ability to answer a range of proportional reasoning based questions and their sense that they can improve and succeed in lessons. So what about an impact within the final exam? You will have seen from the list of topics previously that being able to use a double number line will support students to answer over 25% of a typical paper. We are seeing more of our students do well on these topics, with a growing number using diagrams in the exams.

As one of our students said, "Double number lines make it easier to solve questions. They help me see what I need to do."

Finally, here are a couple of examples of actual exam answers from one of our students who managed to move from a grade 2 to a grade 4 after she became confident using a double number line when she needed it.

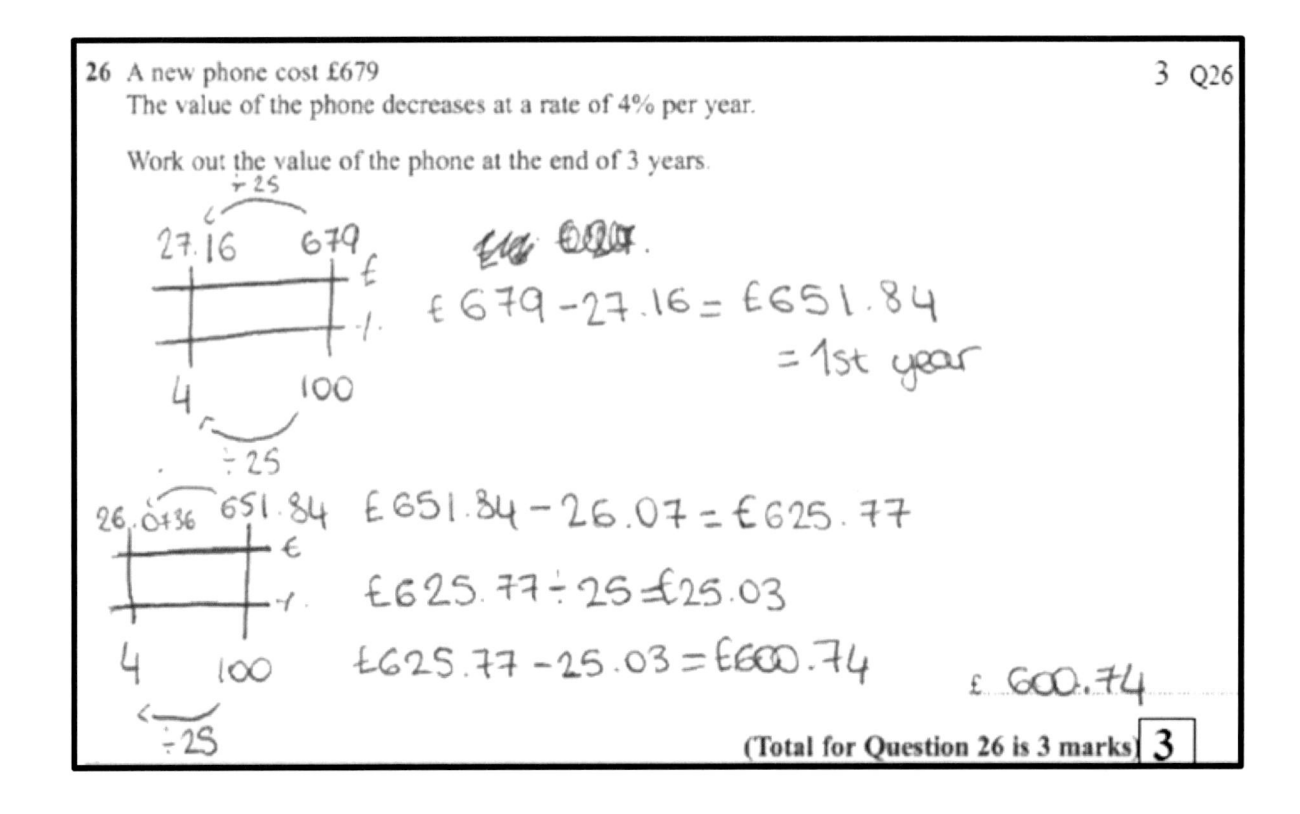

---

26 A new phone cost £679
    The value of the phone decreases at a rate of 4% per year.

    Work out the value of the phone at the end of 3 years.

    £679 − 27.16 = £651.84
    = 1st year

    £651.84 − 26.07 = £625.77
    £625.77 ÷ 25 = £25.03
    £625.77 − 25.03 = £600.74

    £ 600.74

    (Total for Question 26 is 3 marks) 3

---

18 This worked for me!

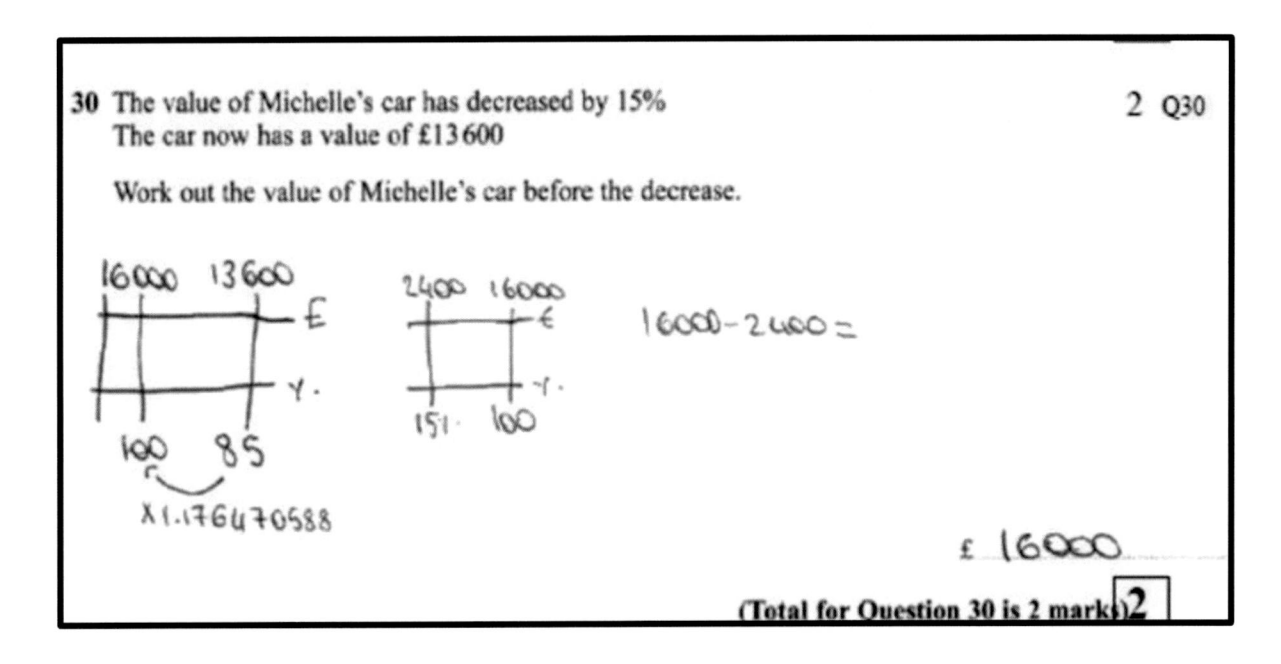

Using double number line to support proportional reasoning

> **30** The value of Michelle's car has decreased by 15%
> The car now has a value of £13 600
>
> Work out the value of Michelle's car before the decrease.
>
> 16000   13600
> ├───┼────┤ £
> ├───┼────┤ %
> 100   85
>   ×1.176470588
>
> 2400   16000
> ├───┼────┤ £
> ├───┼────┤ %
> 15%   100
>
> 16000 − 2400 =
>
> £ 16000
>
> (Total for Question 30 is 2 marks) 2

The use of double number lines in our GCSE Maths teaching has given students a structured picture to support their thinking and develop their understanding, and it has made us and our colleagues think far more carefully about the connections and common structures in the maths that we teach.

---

1 – https://rme.org.uk/
2 – https://www.nottingham.ac.uk/maths-for-life/documents/teacher-resource.pdf

Misunderstandings and misconceptions
Fiona Allan

Fiona has taught all ages from 5 to 18 and, for almost 20 years, worked in a college where she taught Entry level to A-level and also students resitting GCSE Maths.
For the last 18 years, she has worked on many national projects including the Maths Enhancement Programme which upskilled over 2,000 teachers to enable them to teach students resitting GCSE Maths.

When I was teaching students resitting GCSE Maths, I also taught a pre-GCSE class to students who had such a low grade that it was very unlikely they would be able to achieve a pass in one year. After this foundation year, many of them went on to achieve a pass the following year and, indeed, at least one went on to study A-level Maths.

I quickly realised that these students arrived in my class with many misunderstandings and misconceptions which were hampering their progress. I found that once these were resolved by working through the primary syllabus again, they made huge strides and some then did the whole of the secondary syllabus in a remarkably short time. Whilst it isn't possible to spend so much time on the foundations with our GCSE resit students, I found that being aware of their possible misconceptions and misunderstandings really helped me to help them to succeed.

Many things teachers say to primary pupils, which are appropriate at the time, can lead to misconceptions such as:

- You always subtract/take the small number from the big number;
- The more digits there are, the bigger the number;
- To multiply by 10, simply add a 0 to the end of the number;
- To divide by 10, take off the last number and that becomes the remainder; and
- When you multiply two numbers together, you always get a bigger number.

It is so easy to give learners a rule, which works for them at a particular stage in their mathematical thinking, but which will not work as they progress.

Dr Malcolm Swan wrote: "Research has shown that teaching becomes more effective when common mistakes and misconceptions are systematically exposed, challenged and discussed."[1]

I also realised that there are many things we show or tell learners which cause them to infer a rule which is not true, such as:

= means work out the answer

When I started teaching in the college, I was irritated by the number of students who thought that an equals sign means "This is the next thing I thought of/am thinking about".

Reading more about the reasons for this, I found an interesting research paper from *The Mediterranean Journal for Research in Mathematics Education*.[2] "Considering the equal sign as an operator places it in the same class of symbols as the addition, subtraction, multiplication and division signs instead of with other relational symbols such as the greater than (>) and less than (<) signs. This operational interpretation has been considered responsible for functional misconceptions; among them, the one we term "running equal sign" e.g. $2 + 3 = 5 \times 2 = 10 - 2 = 8$.

Capraro et al. argue that young children learn that = means "work out the answer" in Reception classes, if they only meet questions of the type:

$2 + 3 =$
$4 + 5 =$
$7 - 1 =$

The idea that = means "work out the answer", is reinforced when learners use a calculator, when, indeed, pressing the = sign tells the calculator to work out the answer! Capraro et al. write that to overcome the confusion, learners should instead be asked to do calculations such as these:

Complete:

3 + ☐ = 10	10 − ☐ = 3	13 + ☐ = 20	20 − ☐ = 13
☐ + 5 = 10	10 − 5 = ☐	15 + ☐ = 20	20 − ☐ = 15
☐ + ☐ = 10	10 − ☐ = ☐	16 + ☐ = 20	20 − ☐ = 16

Examples from *Teaching for Mastery: Questions, tasks and activities to support assessment*[3]

Fractions – "they're about pizzas, aren't they?"

While observing classes for vocational students resitting GCSE Maths, I was struck by how many teachers used pizzas to explain fractions. Many seem to think that "Pizzas are great for learning about fractions in mathematics. Using basic pizzas, cut them up into halves, quarters etc depending on the fractions being taught. You can use them very effectively to do simple fractions or to do mixed or improper fractions. Visually the children can easily identify that seven quarters make one whole and three quarters. They are also very good for doing addition and subtraction of fractions too and if you're feeling really brave division of fractions where you might have four pizzas divided into sixths so twenty four sixths and share these between six people, they'd have four sixths (or maybe visually two thirds) of a pizza each. This makes maths (and the tricky and potentially dull topic of fractions) exciting and motivational for the children and will guarantee that the lesson, and hopefully its objectives, will stay in their minds."[4] And many online games about fractions are based around pizzas.

But thinking of fractions as part of a circle makes understanding a fraction as part of a whole more difficult. If we start thinking that a fraction is part of a whole pizza, does it make it difficult for us to think of, say, how many learners are in a quarter of a class, where the "whole" can change depending on how many learners there are each day?

Every maths teacher who has not yet read the NCETM's *Preparing for fractions: the part-whole relationship*[5] should do so. Here the focus is on "identifying a whole and part of a whole in different contexts, as well as exploring some aspects of these, for example, whether the parts within the whole are equal or unequal, and the relative size of a part and a whole."

"The word 'fraction', however, is not used within the segment at all by the children and at no point do they write using fractional notation, e.g. 1/4 , or verbalise the names of any fractions (for example, 'one quarter'). This may seem to be moving very slowly, but spending time looking at the relative sizes of parts and wholes gets to the crux of the proportional aspect of the fraction."

The number system starts at 0 or 1

Most number lines seen in younger pupils' classrooms start at 0 or 1. A number line starting at 1 creates a further problem almost immediately because under the National Curriculum for Key Stage 1, for example, children should be taught to:

- recognise, find and name a half as one of two equal parts of an object, shape or quantity; and
- recognise, find, name a quarter as one of four equal parts of an object, shape or quantity.

If the number line in the classroom, starts at 1, where do ½ and ¼ fit on the number line?

Until recently, we tended to assume that young children understood the meaning of zero in the UK. Some years ago, I watched a Chinese teacher from Shanghai spend a lesson teaching a class of 5-year-olds the meaning of zero. The consensus of the British teachers observing the lesson was that none of them had ever thought of teaching their pupils such a lesson, they "assumed" that young children understood the meaning of zero. The Chinese teacher explained that we shouldn't make this assumption.

Do we tell learners that there are numbers to the left (or smaller) than zero and numbers bigger than (the largest number on our number line) saying, for example, "You don't know about them yet, but you will learn about them in the future"?

All hexagons (or pentagons or octagons etc.) have equal sides

From the moment that young children are introduced to shapes, they encounter regular sided shapes when they are given one of those posting box games as a toddler. If you buy a poster of 2D shapes for your classroom wall, it is likely that it will only feature regular shapes. So it is probably not surprising that I found questions like this being asked online by adults:

- "What do I call an irregular quadrilateral with 6 sides?"
- "What is an irregular 8-sided shape called?"
- "Can I call a 6-sided polygon a 'hexagon' even if the sides aren't equal?"

While we understandably focus on regular shapes, I also tried to show my classes pictures of irregular ones as well.

Triangles

When asked about triangle a), some learners will say that it has two sides and a "bottom" and that, triangle b) has two sides and a "top" and that only triangle c) has three sides.

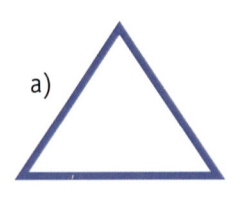

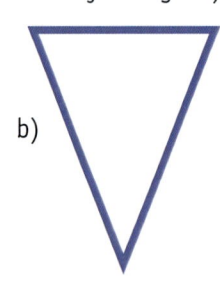

Similarly, many believe that only triangles like d) or e) can be called right-angled triangles because they rarely see right-angled triangle such as f).

This is true of many shapes and students can misname shapes which have a corner rather than a side at the bottom.

Questions like this one, challenge learners to identify shapes which aren't "the usual way up".

Identify the regular and irregular quadrilaterals

Example from *Teaching for Mastery: Questions, tasks and activities to support assessment*[6]

Equations never have a negative sign before them

I saw that in the many textbooks in our department and in the worksheets my colleagues wrote, almost none of the equations had a negative sign at the beginning. I rarely found an equation which had a minus sign at the start e.g. $- 20x + 26 + 6 = 34$.

Allegedly, until recently, it was very difficult for typesetters to have a minus sign at the beginning of an algebraic equation/expression and so there were very few, if any, examples with minus signs before equations/expressions, in textbooks or exam papers. So children start to think that, if, they, for example, multiply out $(- 2a + 3b)(4a + b)$ and get the answer $- 8a^2 + 10ab + 3b^2$, they have got the wrong answer. I have taught students resitting GCSE, who ignored any minus signs at the beginning of algebraic expressions and equations even when their own workings had resulted in an expression or equation with a minus sign at the beginning.

Conclusion

I quickly realised that I needed to change my practice. I had to give the students activities which made them confront their beliefs such as this one from *Improving learning in mathematics*[7]:

N2 Card set A – *Statements*

$3 + x = x + 3$ It doesn't matter which way round you add, you get the same answer.	$2 - x = x - 2$ It doesn't matter which way round you subtract, you get the same answer.
$5 \times x = x \times 5$ It doesn't matter which way round you multiply, you get the same answer.	$x \div 2 = 2 \div x$ It doesn't matter which way round you divide, you get the same answer.
$5 + x > 5$ If you add a number to 5, your answer will be more than 5.	$x + 8 > x$ If you add 8 to a number, your answer will be more than the number.
$5 - x \leq 5$ If you take a number away from 5, your answer will be less than or equal to 5.	$x - 10 > x$ If you take 10 away from a number, the answer will be greater than the number.
$4x \geq 4$ If you multiply 4 by a number, your answer will be greater than or equal to 4.	$10x \geq x$ If you multiply 10 by a number, your answer will be greater than or equal to the number.
$\frac{x}{2} < x$ If you divide a number by 2, the answer will be less than the number.	$\frac{10}{x} \leq 10$ If you divide 10 by a number, your answer will be less than or equal to 10.
$\sqrt{x} \leq x$ The square root of a number is less than or equal to the number.	$x^2 \geq x$ The square of a number is greater than or equal to the number.

N2 • Evaluating statements about number operations

And I was aware that I had to be careful how I drew triangles and other diagrams on the board.

Overall, helping my FE students sort out their misunderstandings and misconceptions enabled them to make progress in maths, sometimes for the first time in their lives.

Most of this chapter was originally published in Equals Online - Mathematics and Special Educational Needs.

Further Reading

Children's Errors in Mathematics, Edited by Alice Hansen, pub. 2005

---

1 – *Improving learning in mathematics: challenges and strategies, 2005* https://colleenyoung.files.wordpress.com/2010/04/improving_learning_in_mathematicsi.pdf

2 – Capraro, R. M., Capraro, M. M., Yetkiner, Z. E., Corlu, M. S., Ozel, S., Ye, S., & Kim, H. G. (2011). An international perspective between problem types in textbooks and students' understanding of relational equality. Mediterranean Journal for Research in Mathematics Education: An International Journal, 10, 187-213.

3 – https://www.ncetm.org.uk/media/qjpctp24/mastery_assessment_y1.pdf

4 – https://freedomtoteach.collins.co.uk/primary-maths-pizza-fractions/

5 – https://www.ncetm.org.uk/media/1qyn40y1/ncetm_spine3_segment01_y3.pdf

6 – https://www.ncetm.org.uk/media/lp0o2lgv/mastery_assessment_y5.pdf

7 – https://www.stem.org.uk/resources/elibrary/resource/26920/evaluating-statements-about-number-operations-n2

The use of the Socratic method to foster discussion

Despoina Boli

Despoina has over 12 years of experience teaching mathematics and has spent the last seven years working at a central London Further Education college, where her focus has been on resit learners. For the past two years, she has been the curriculum manager for Functional Skills and GCSE Mathematics.

It is widely recognised that teaching learners who are resitting GCSE Maths is a challenging task. When I first started working in Further Education (FE) seven years ago, I was shocked by the low level of contributions and exchange of ideas within my lessons. After discussing this with colleagues, I realised that this was the norm in a resit class. Learners seemed to lack the motivation and enthusiasm needed to actively participate in maths discussions. I vividly remember that, at times, I would pose a question and none of the learners would attempt to respond or even ask for clarifications. I had to find a way to change the nature of my lessons.

To me, the element of interaction between the teacher and the learners, as well as among the learners themselves in a classroom, is essential. I dedicated a lot of time to researching engaging strategies and effective questioning techniques until I came across the Socratic method. I believed this method could help me create a classroom environment in which learners would feel capable of discussing, contributing and enhancing their understanding and proficiency in GCSE Maths.

Using a sequence of inquiries, the ancient Greek philosopher Plato employs Socrates to unveil the ideas of his conversational partner by restating, reconstructing, or elaborating upon them further. The Socratic method is known for its meticulous examination of the arguments being scrutinised. At the core of this process lies the art of dialogue. Within his dialogues, Socrates pretends to lack knowledge about a particular subject, aiming to gain a comprehensive understanding of the topic from another person. Through logical reasoning, he endeavours to expose any misunderstandings and bring to light inconsistencies and contradictions within the position of his conversational partner. Socrates doesn't position himself as the authority in these dialogues; rather, he intends to assist the individuals in identifying their own flawed reasoning or further develop their arguments.

This is the fundamental concept behind the method. To apply it effectively in my lessons, I had to tailor it to suit the context of GCSE Maths. As I understood it, the method entails using a series of questions that can steer learners towards enhancing their comprehension of mathematical problems and refining their communication skills. My primary objective was to motivate learners to rely less on the teacher and improve their abilities in problem-solving and reasoning through dialogues and discussions.

The initial stage of implementation involved designing each lesson and incorporating opportunities for questioning that would foster dialogue. I came across a website[1] that aided me to further comprehend the method, and another one that provided me with question ideas specifically tailored for maths[2]. In the first year, I spent my time planning lessons and then reflecting on them to enhance subsequent sessions. It was a process I greatly enjoyed, as it also deepened my subject knowledge and offered insights into the misconceptions my learners had developed from prior experiences. The second year, I participated in a lesson study with two other colleagues and a coach who helped us refine the method within our teaching practice. That year, we also sought feedback from our learners to have a holistic view of the approach.

The six types of Socratic questions that can be used interchangeably are the following:

1. Questions that clarify;
2. Questions that challenge assumptions;
3. Questions that examine evidence or reasons;
4. Questions about viewpoints and perspectives;
5. Questions that explore implications and consequences; and
6. Questions about the question.

Below, you will see an example of Socratic dialogue that took place in one of my revision sessions, involving myself and five learners. The dialogue is focusing on the first part of the problem and shows how I incorporated the elements of Socratic questioning in my teaching. The day before, learners had gone through the steps of solving different types of equations so the aim of that session was to focus on the forming of an equation and making connections with other topics. In my experience, resit learners often memorise steps and facts, but face challenges when it comes to applying them in more complex probl ems. My intention was to help learners rectify their misconceptions, familiarise them with mathematical terminology, and facilitate the development of mathematical reasoning.

Shown below is an isosceles triangle. Each side is measured in centimetres.

Work out the area of the triangle.

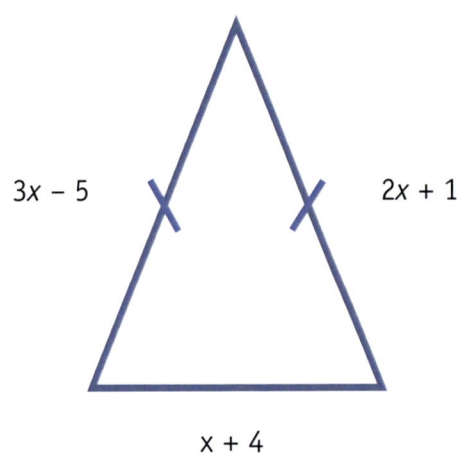

$3x - 5$ $2x + 1$

$x + 4$

Teacher: So, what do you see here?

Student A: A triangle.

Teacher: What kind of triangle is it?

Student A: An isosceles triangle.

Teacher: Can someone tell me what the word "isosceles" means?

Student B: Two of the sides are equal?

Teacher: Yes, two of the sides are equal! Let's see what problem is here. What does the question ask us to find out?

Student C: To find the length of the base.

Teacher: Ok! And which side on this triangle is the base?

Student C: The $x + 4$, I think...

Teacher: Do you all agree? (Most of the students nodding). What do we need to know to be able to work out the length of the base, so, the $x + 4$? (Students look at the triangle and think). So, any suggestions? What information is missing to be able to find the length of the base?

Student C: We don't know what x is.

Teacher: Is there any way we can work out the value of x?

Student C: Probably, yes?

Teacher: How can we work out the value of x?

Student D: Is it the thing when we make an equation?

Teacher: Good observation! How can we make an equation in this case? Remember what you know about this triangle!

Student D: Should we add them all together? Then we get $6x$?

Teacher: Is "$6x$" an equation?

Student. D: Yes...??

Teacher: Could someone give me an example of an equation?

Student E: $2x - 3 = 8$?

Teacher: What is the difference between "$6x$" and "$2x - 3 = 8$"?

Student C: The equal (=)?

Teacher: Exactly! The equals sign! So, something must be equal to something else, right? So, "$6x$" is an algebraic expression and "$2x - 3 = 8$" is an equation.

Students: Yes (some nodding)

Teacher: If you ever get confused, think of the word "equation", the word "equal" is hidden in it. Let's get back to our question. Do we have anything to be equal to something else in this problem?

Student D: A triangle adds up to 180, right?

Teacher: So when you say, "A triangle adds up...", what do you mean? What exactly in the triangle that adds up to 180?

Student D: Ehmm... the angles?

Teacher: Good, the angles. Do we have any information about any of the angles in this triangle?

Student D: No...

Teacher: So, although you are right, angles in a triangle do add up to 180 degrees, can we use it to form an equation, in this question?

Student D: I don't think so.

Teacher: Have a moment and observe your triangle and the information given to you so far. What could help you to form an equation?

Student B: The two sides of the triangle are equal, no?

Teacher: Correct! We already know that the triangle is isosceles. Can you form an equation from that?

Student B: Is it like .... $3x - 5 + 2x + 1$???

Teacher: Think of what you said a minute ago, "two sides are equal", did you use the word add?

Student B: hmmm...so, $3x - 5 = 2x + 1$?

Teacher: Do you all agree? Does this sound correct? (Some students hesitate but eventually all agree on $3x - 5 = 2x + 1$). Let's solve it then and find the value of x. I will give you a few minutes to solve it, you can work with each other. (Students solve the equation). So, what is the value of x?

Student E: I got 6?

Teacher: Would you like to show everyone how you solved it on the board? (Student solves the equation and talks through the steps) Do you all agree with your classmate?

Students: Yes!

Teacher: So, are we done now?

    Student E: Yeah, I think so...

    Student C: Don't we have to work out the length of the base?

Teacher: Yes, we do! How do we do that?

    Student C: Well, we know that x is 6, so 6 + 4 is 10. The base is 10.

Teacher: 10 what?

    Student C: 10cm.

Teacher: Great, that's it! Let's do the second part of the problem now.

The dialogue above is only an example and reflecting on it, I would probably change my questioning in parts or I would have tried to step out for a bit and let the learners lead. There will always be space for improvement. Through my experience, I have observed the power of the method to transform traditional teaching dynamics and empower students to approach complex problems with confidence. Acknowledging the inherent challenges in teaching GCSE Maths to resit learners, this method offers a dynamic solution to foster engagement and comprehension, and equips them with tools that extend beyond rote memorisation. However, I won't deny that it took me a minimum of two years to cultivate a profound understanding of how to effectively implement it in my daily teaching routine and begin observing positive outcomes among my learners. Trial and error, meticulous planning, and reflective practices are pivotal elements in refining the development of this method.

---

1 – *https://argoprep.com/blog/using-socratic-method-in-your-classroom/*

2 – *https://madmimi.com/s/105746*

Daily Maths
Julia Smith

Julia is a National Maths Teacher Trainer and an author with BBC Bitesize, Cambridge University Press, Oxford University Press and Collins, a member of the AQA Experts Panel and the author of the post-16 maths area on AQA All About Maths. Julia is also Creator and Project Lead on the EEF Research Trial of the 5Rs Resit Curriculum and a Shine Teachers Award Winner.

Your resit or functional maths learners have seen all of the maths before. If they have any GCSE Maths grade and have attended the vast majority of primary and secondary maths classes then they do know a lot of maths - probably enough to gain a grade 4, but they are carrying a wide variety of misconceptions and misunderstandings. So, a resit year or functional maths programme can be a revision year. This means that there can be a very different emphasis and approach than if they were any other cohort of learners.

The only way to get good at maths, is to do maths. It's a bit like playing football or learning to knit - the only way to get really good at it and, by that, I mean fast and efficient, is to practise, practise, practise.

Practise until you cannot get it wrong, not just until you get it right

Ask any learner how they get good at anything – cooking, singing, swimming, netball – they will tell you about training sessions and practice on a regular basis.

Maths is good for you: it's like 5 fruit and veg a day, running, 10,000 steps a day. We may not like it and it may require having a little word with yourself to get started. Unfortunately, a lot of our learners do not realise the benefits of being good at maths.

National Numeracy tell us that learners with a good maths grade will earn more over their lifetime at work than those without and it will look great on any CV.

So tell them the stories of learners like them. Tell them of Lauren Reid who passed her GCSE Maths resit after 9 attempts; 29 year old Jess Ward, who needed a GCSE Maths grade 4 to start teacher training and who passed thirteen years after leaving school and after four attempts. Talk to them about resilience, tenacity and persistence. Find examples that are meaningful to your learners.

Grade 4 Maths will open doors that learners don't even realise are shut yet

National Numeracy talks about three things – **valuing** the qualification, **belief** that you can do it second, third time around and putting some **effort** in. Your learners have a much better chance of gaining that grade 4, if not a grade 5, or that Functional Skill pass if they put some effort in, outside of the classroom - on the bus, in the staffroom at work, over lunch at college.

Dylan Wiliam tells us a key to success is to: *"Make the students the architect of their own learning."*

This means involving them in planning their learning and choice in what mechanisms to use. If they take ownership of the revision and make decisions in what and how to work then they are more likely to actually do it.

So how do we get learners to put some effort in and engage our resit and functional maths learners in some Daily Maths?

Revise the maths – see the maths differently second time around

If you turn your programme into a revision-based approach then to revise means to revisit maths topics regularly; to recall key facts and figures; to re-vision the maths by looking at a variety of media to help in the revision process.

Discuss with learners about revising:

- How to revise;
- When to revise;
- Where to revise;
- What to revise; and
- Who could they revise with?

The fact that learners may already have a maths grade is a good starting point.

- Find out what they can do and strengthen that;
- Find out what they "sort of know" and plug the gaps; and
- Find out what they don't know and leave that until later.

The nine maths basics – addition, subtraction, multiplication, division, fractions, decimals, percentages, scale and ratio – are the cornerstones of maths, and that is the best starting point, given the hierarchical nature of maths. Find out what they can do in these topics and what their misunderstandings and misconceptions are and help them to sort this out and then build on these foundation skills.

Homework: traditionally our learners go home but they don't work

More commonly, they go off to a shift at work (such are money pressures) or they are disadvantaged with other pressures or have a learning need. So the last thing they may have on their mind is some maths homework.

Instead of homework why not try pre-work. This is when you tell learners what is coming up next. Give them some ideas of how to prepare for this: things to read, things to watch.

For example, "Next week we are looking at all things Pythagoras and Pythagoras' Theorem. Take a look at *BBC Bitesize*[1] or *Corbettmaths*[2]." YouTube channels like *Mr Morley Maths*[3] or *GCSE Maths Tutor*[4] may also be something learners might like to look at before the next class. Usually, adult learners like this approach as it can give a bit of confidence and it's an opportunity for the learner to get slightly ahead of their peers.

If you can't beat them, join them. In this modern age learners spend an inordinate amount of time on Tik Tok, YouTube and Instagram. This may not be an area of resource that we feel too comfortable with ourselves but it shouldn't be dismissed because it can be a valuable support area. One thing you could ask learners to do at the start of your course, is to make some recommendations of channels and people to follow for maths support, in the spirit of Dylan Wiliam's idea of making the learner the architect of their own learning. There are some excellent sites out there - take a look for yourself. There are also some shockers so be prepared to guide learners to the quality areas. Some post-16 providers also have their own Tik Tok or Instagram accounts that learners can tap into outside of class.

Homework is not an assessment opportunity. Anything that requires a learner to log in with a username and password will not prove popular; nor should it be used as a monitoring device. Homework, pre-work or daily maths should simply be a practice and consolidation opportunity; doing it because they see the benefit it will bring because you have sold it as such, from the start.

Anytime, anyplace, anywhere learning - get busy on the bus!

Building good habits from Day 1 of your course by promoting areas of maths that learners can easily engage with, will pay dividends. Giving them access to maths games – of which there are a plethora – and encouraging them to play these to develop their maths fluency will strengthen what they already know and get them into good habits. Websites like *Transum Games*[5], Tom Scott's *"You can't do simple maths under pressure*"[6] and various Times Tables apps are vital and they don't require a log-in. Maybe you prefer something like *Corbettmaths* 5-a-day[7] or *Mathsbot* Number of the Day[8]. It's purely a practice opportunity or "training session" that learners will benefit from, in terms of maths fluency. A little bit of maths a day, just 15 to 20 minutes, will have a big impact on success.

What does mathematical fluency mean? If you are fluent in another language then it means you don't have to think too much about it; it comes quickly and naturally. One memorable learner said that being fluent in another language means that "You even dream in that language". That is what we want ideally for our learners; that they have a level of fluency which does not hinder the harder thinking required.

Nor does it impact upon working memory. For example, if a problem requires the learner to calculate 9×8 within it, then being able to do that quickly and efficiently means that it won't detract from the bigger problem. Conversely, if the learner gets bogged down in calculating 9×8, they will have less time to spend on the larger problem as well as some probable mounting pressure and stress. Daily Maths and maths games will strengthen mathematical fluency.

Colin Foster tells us that success in problem solving is reliant upon mathematical fluency and reasoning. You won't be good at the former without the latter.

Practice may not make perfect - but it may make permanent

Celebrate success. Find the learner who is "busy on the bus", doing a little bit of maths every day. Make a fuss of them and tell them how much this means in terms of chances of future success. Make sure that others in the group can hear this too. It's not often that a 17 year old welder gets told they are doing brilliantly, and success can build success – a coaching strategy - as others want a slice of the praise. Give out a silly sticker, put a gold star on some great work, this may seem very patronising but I have seen many a health and social care learner ask for a Peppa Pig sticker when they have done some good work! Don't knock it if it motivates!

Remember that whilst across the board high grade outcomes are traditionally low, for every learner that achieves that grade 4 GCSE Maths resit or their L2 Functional Maths qualification, it is 100% success for them!

---

1 – *https://www.bbc.co.uk/bitesize/subjects/z38pycw*

2 – *https://corbettmaths.com/*

3 – *https://www.youtube.com/@MorleyMaths*

4 – *https://www.youtube.com/@TheGCSEMathsTutor*

5 – *https://www.transum.org/Software/Game/*

6 – *https://www.tomscott.com/usvsth3m/maths/*

7 – *https://corbettmaths.com/5-a-day/gcse/*

8 – *https://mathsbot.com/starters/numberOfTheDay*

Language in the resit GCSE Maths classroom

Jenny Stacey

Jenny Stacey taught maths in an East Midlands FE college from 2004 until 2022. She has taught Key Skills, Basic Skills, ESOL maths, Functional Skills, and GCSE to adults and 16- to 18-year-olds, including ESOL/EAL students. Currently she is employed as an Associate Lecturer at Sheffield Hallam University.

What works for me when teaching GCSE Mathematics in FE classrooms? Well, for me, it is particular attention to the language, certainly for ESOL/EAL students, but also for everyone in maths classrooms in FE. Whether you have students whose first language is or is not English, if students cannot understand the question, they will be put off from engaging with it, and having the confidence to engage is perhaps one of the first steps in the process of improving grades.

I have several examples of what works for me in this chapter. These include the different words that we have in English which attach to the symbols for the four number operations, +, -, x and ÷, using both a poster format and matching activities. I also advocate the use of a display board for key definitions of maths terms during lessons, often including words that have more than one meaning in English, such as table and change. Finally, there is a reminder about the language of command words used by different exam boards, and the need to use the same language in resources and classroom discussions.

Words for number operations

Question: How many words are there for the four basic number operations in English?

Answer: Loads!

Often many more than are present in other languages, for instance:

Addition: add, plus, altogether, and, sum, total (students also need to understand more than);

Subtraction: subtract, take away, minus, difference between (and less than);

Multiplication: multiply, product, of (as in what is half of 8? ½ x 8 = 4), times, expand; and

Division: divide, share, share by, split, remainder, factorise.

You may be able to add others to this list. Some of these words are confusing for learners, such as "product", which can be confused with items that are made, or what you put on your hair in the morning, and "times", which can get confused with times table grids. "Take away" can be especially troublesome, as it has very different alternative meaning! On the plus side (forgive the pun!), plus and minus are quite common, although you will find different pronunciations.

The English words for number operations do not always translate easily for those EAL/ESOL learners, who may have other words in their own languages, such as in Italian, "remove" is used to signify subtraction, and most English words when translated are not used, but in English "remove" is not usual.

In my first solution for this challenge, I use four pieces of A3 paper and put the symbol in the middle of a circle at the centre, so +, −, × and ÷. I then divide the page into as many sections as needed to cover everyone's languages, including English, so it looks like rays of the sun. I put all the English words in the top section and ask the representatives of the different languages to fill in their part, with a note of which language it is, and a drawing of the symbol if it is different. This is important, because most languages do not use the division symbol as it is used in for instance, the UK, USA, Australia, New Zealand, and Sweden, they use the symbol ":". As this symbol is used in the UK for ratios, this can cause a lot of confusion.

The production of a poster which shows the differences between languages can improve respect in the classroom. In my classroom we have had English, French, Spanish, Italian, Bulgarian, Russian, Lithuanian, Ethiopian, Chinese, Arabic and Urdu on display, which reminds those who do speak English, or who are familiar with the Romanised alphabet, how much harder it might be for those with a language where the script is very different, and may not even be written in the same direction, from left to right, as is used in English.

The second solution is a matching activity of words and the four number operations, like the one shown below, completed by students working in twos or threes. Matching activities can encourage debate and discussion, and act as an "ice breaker" perceived as relevant to the students.

Example of a matching activity using symbols and words

Matching activities for sentences with number operations

The next example of what works for me is a great follow up to the first examples, as I use a matching activity of sentences and answers, which use all the different words that you might find in English. I usually split these into the four number operations, so that students are aware that they are dealing with one number operation at a time, and ask the students to tackle them in pairs or small groups. This is another great ice breaker and gets students working together.

For example, the addition pack might contain sentences such as "What is 34 and seven altogether?", which checks for whether the words for numbers are understood in addition to the sum. One of the answers in the pack is "41" on a separate card, so students have to match the phrases to the answers. You might want to use the word form of some numbers to mix it up a bit. The addition pack might seem easy, but it enables you to discuss with the whole class the two different ways that "sum" and "total" are used, as we do any sum we will get a total, or answer, but if we "sum 3 and 4" or "total 3 and 4", we are being asked to add.

In English, the numbers are not necessarily in the same order in the sentences all the time, which can confuse both English speakers and others. For instance, one card could say "subtract 7 from 14", whilst another says, "what is 14 minus 7?" These have the same answer, but the order in the sentence is different. In my experience it is very common for students to change the sum around if it makes it easier, such as "what is 11 minus 12?". The answer I am often given is 1, but it should be –1 (minus 1). I always have an example like this in the subtraction pack, so that I can discuss this response with students!

Of course, with addition and multiplication calculations, the order the numbers appear in does not matter, because these calculations are commutative, but subtraction and division are non-commutative, so these questions must be read carefully. It can help students to be aware of this, although they might not use the words "commutative" or "non-commutative".

In each pack I include an error, which I alert students to, because this will speed up my ability to visit each group in the room and assess whether they have completed the task correctly or not. Each group should be showing me a card that does not match a question or is incorrect for some reason before they can move onto the next pack. For instance, in the addition pack there is a transposition, which gives me an opportunity to talk about how common it is for many of our learners to either make a transposition when they make a calculation, or when they move their answer onto the answer line, either of which could result in lost marks on an exam paper.

An example of one of the addition packs is shown below. The transposition is in 18,632, as the answer should be 18,362! Not all students will use commas in number strings, by the way; the computer version of this is to leave a gap, and in most European countries the comma and decimal point are swapped, so 18,362 could look like 18 point 362 to some of the ESL students.

Example of a matching activity for addition questions

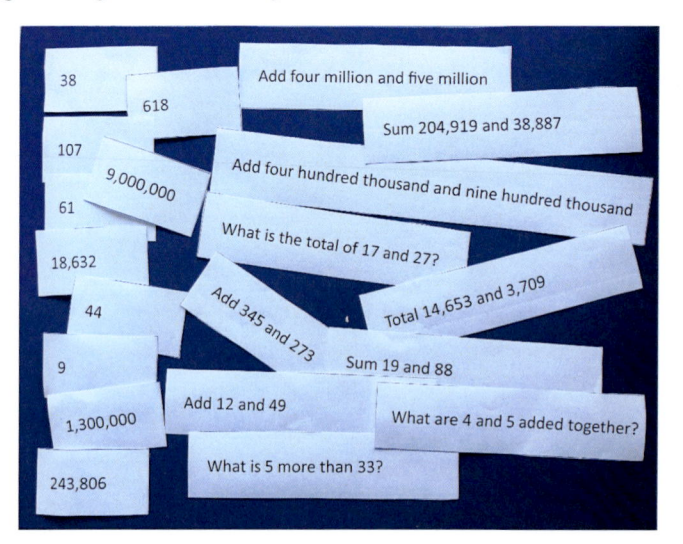

Definitions of maths words on display

The third idea that I have, which I use throughout the maths courses, is that I put key words with their definitions up on the board in all sessions, apart from those sessions which include assessments.

For instance, if I want students to learn about averages calculations, I will display the definitions of mean, median, mode, (or modal value), and range so that all students can refer to them during the lesson if they need to. This can benefit all students regardless of their first language, as it is easy to get the "three ms" muddled, and displaying key definitions can reduce the cognitive load of those who are practising calculations, which encourages engagement and helps to improve confidence.

Other words with specific maths meanings, such as "integer" and "circumference" are not easily retained by all students if they are used infrequently, or not at all, outside of the maths classroom. A poster display of definitions of these terms can really help.

Words with more than one meaning in English

Some words have a normal meaning, and a maths meaning, and I highlight these to my students when we meet them, such as the word "product" already discussed. An excellent example of another word is "change" because it has so many meanings, such as to change one's clothes, or have a change of heart, but is also used for how much money is returned to me when I give a shop assistant more money than is needed for my purchase.

"Table" is another word whose definitions may need clarifying, and "pound" another.

Unfamiliar contexts

I check for understanding of other words that are not understood by everyone as we progress through the lesson and put those up too. For instance, those studying hairdressing might be unfamiliar with the ratios of ingredients in a mortar mix, although they would be very familiar with those in hair dye. Students whose first language is not English might have little or no experience of either context in English.

Some students can reject engaging with a question because they are unfamiliar with the context, for example, I once heard a student disengage from a question phrased in the language of football, because they did not "know anything about football"!

Command words used by exam boards

The last example of something that works for me is focusing on the language of exam boards. Exam boards have different ways of giving instructions to students, known as command words.

Examples include "calculate", which at least one exam board has recently changed to "work out" on its papers; "solve", which might be written as "find a value for x"; "expand", which may be written as "multiply out". One exam board has just moved from "convert" when asking students to convert, say, metres to centimetres, to "change". Yet another use of the word "change"!

It is really important to have a clear understanding of the language used by the exam board and to use it in lessons, so that the students are familiar with the commands they are likely to meet. I check this every year because exam boards seem to be reviewing the command words they use regularly. It is worth enquiring if your exam board will send you a poster for display.

Finally

So, there you have it, examples of the aspects of language that can cause confusion and dismay for students, with solutions that have worked for me, both with 16- to 18-year-olds and adults, and with both students who have English as their first language and those who have learned English as their second or third (or fourth) language.

Further reading

Stacey, J. M. (2016). Does adding Mathematics to English language learners' timetables improve their acquisition of English? *Language Issues 27.1*, 84-87.

Stacey, J. M. (2017, June 17). Mathematics and Examination Anxiety in Adult Learners: the findings of surveys of GCSE Maths students in an FE college in the UK. *All Hands on Math Proceedings of the 24th International Conference of Adults Learning Mathematics* (pp. 113-121). Rotterdam: *alm-online.net*. Retrieved from Adults Learning Mathematics: *http://www.alm-online.net/wp-content/uploads/2016/12/ALM24-Stacey_Jenny-Mathematics-and-Examination-Anxiety-in-Adult-Learners.pdf*

Stacey, J. M. (2018). How language interferes with maths: a guide for teachers of ESOL mathematics. *Language Issues Volume 29.1*, 45-53.

Stacey, J. M. (Feb 2022). Changing perceptions among adult learners (19+) in further education studying GCSE mathematics: Methodology and data analysis -the importance of the pilot. *Twelfth Congress of the European Society for Research in Mathematics Education (CERME12)* (pp. 1-8). Bozen-Bolzano, Italy: *https://hal.science/CERME12/hal-03745546v1*

Non-mathematical starters

Despoina Boli

Despoina has over 12 years of experience teaching mathematics and has spent the last seven years working at a central London Further Education college, where her focus has been on resit learners. For the past two years, she has been the curriculum manager for Functional Skills and GCSE Mathematics.

Our classrooms are not just spaces for disseminating knowledge, but also platforms for connecting with the diverse tapestry of learners whom we meet every year. For successful teaching and learning outcomes, it is essential to understand the experiences and aspirations that shape our learners beyond the realm of our classroom. This chapter explores a different approach I call *non-mathematical starters*, a strategy that seeks to unearth the layers of personal stories that our students carry with them.

Over the last decade, there has been significant interest in understanding the characteristics of resit learners and the factors that bring them to our resit classes. Through both experience and research studies, we have come to understand that a considerable portion of our learners exhibit a lack of motivation, an aversion to mathematics, a history of repeated failures, limited engagement with the subject, and are likely not to have chosen to resit maths if that were an option. Nonetheless, I was always wondering what prompts these learners to adopt such attitudes. What narratives lay beneath their experiences? By initiating discussions that transcend numbers and equations, we open a gateway to understanding their journeys - why they resit maths, what dreams propel them forward, and what challenges they strive to overcome.

For the whole Autumn term, I take an unconventional approach to starting our classroom sessions. Instead of immediately delving into mathematical challenges, I focus on personal reflections. I ask questions about their past experiences with maths, the teachers who've made an impact, and the obstacles they have faced. These questions provide insights into why they are here resitting maths. I also ask about their favourite songs, not just to create a positive atmosphere, but to uncover their unique personalities. I ask about their travel aspirations, drawing parallels between their dreams and the vast world. These seemingly unrelated topics lay the groundwork for a classroom environment that values empathy and recognition. As time goes on, these non-mathematical discussions become bridges that build trust and understanding. Their responses give me a glimpse into their characters. This approach helps me adapt my teaching methods, incorporating their passions and goals into their maths lessons.

To me, the resit journey isn't just about tackling maths concepts. It is also a journey of self-discovery. As educators, our role goes beyond teaching formulas and calculations. It involves recognising each learner's unique story. By starting with these non-mathematical conversations, I hope to establish trust and connections, creating an environment where students feel acknowledged and valued. Let me now introduce you to the structure and purpose of these non-mathematical starters.

At the start of every lesson, as learners enter the classroom, I have already prepared one or two non-mathematical questions on the board. On each desk, I have placed a sheet of paper with the same questions. Learners are instructed to write down the date and their name on the paper, and then spend the next ten minutes answering the questions. Following this, they are given the opportunity to share their responses with the entire class if they choose to do so. At the end of the activity, I gather their answers and place them in their individual folders after the lesson.

Below are some examples of the questions I tend to ask:

- Do you recall any of your previous maths teachers?
- What aspects of mathematics do you enjoy, and which do you dislike?
- What are your expectations from your maths teacher?
- What are your goals for this academic year?
- What are some of your favourite songs?

- Where would you like to travel, and what is the reason behind your choice?
- What course are you currently studying in college? What motivated you to select this course?
- Could you share a happy memory of yours?
- Do you have any favourite podcasts, movies, series or TV shows that you enjoy?
- How do you typically approach studying for maths exams or assessments?
- Are there any hobbies or interests that you do outside of college that you would like to share?
- Is there a specific maths skill that you would like to improve this year?
- What kind of support do you find most helpful when learning maths?
- Do you have any favourite quotes that inspire you?
- Are there any cultural traditions or festivals that hold significance for you?

As you can see, there are two kinds of questions: those related to their relationship and experiences with mathematics and those related to personal interests. I usually have two sessions per week with each of my groups, posing a different type of question for each session. This approach gives me the opportunity to get to know my learners, understand what each one brings in my classroom, and cultivate a classroom environment of mutual trust. I also engage by answering the same questions and sharing my responses. After class, I take time to review their answers, considering that some prefer not to share during class. Furthermore, I use their responses related to their interests to develop context for maths problems and the ones related to experiences with mathematics to modify my teaching methods if needed. The question about favourite songs, for example, I use to create a playlist of songs which plays in the background during group work.

One challenge I have encountered relates to learners sharing their responses. During the first few weeks, most learners are reluctant about speaking up in front of the class. However, as they become more familiar with each other, this hesitation decreases. To help with the process, I demonstrate that I read their responses by commenting on what they wrote on a one-to-one basis. I believe that this shows them that I care about their thoughts and that I take their responses seriously. After a few weeks, learners know what they are expected to do when they arrive in class.

Sometimes I repeat the questions about the learners' mathematical experiences during the spring term. I then compare their responses to those given the first time and check for any differences. This is a valuable way to gather feedback on their current experiences with learning mathematics.

Engaging our students on a personal level fosters an environment where trust takes root and genuine relationships flourish. By tailoring our teaching to their unique stories, we are able to adapt our methods and also convey a respect for their individuality. The journey of understanding our students is an ongoing one, marked by the willingness to listen and the desire to connect. Non-mathematical starters have proven to be more than just a tool; they are a testament to the power of empathy and the art of teaching beyond numbers.

Engaging real-world investigations

Martin Newton

After working in agriculture and horticulture and running his own business, Martin returned to an FE college, where he sat GCSEs and A levels before taking a BEd Hons in Mathematics. Martin worked in three colleges before becoming a Mathematics Education Support Specialist with a national charity improving maths education.

When I think back over my career as a maths teacher in Further Education teaching GCSE and a range of maths courses to 16+ students including adults, I realise that I always wanted to put things into a real-world context. This was rooted in my previous careers where I used maths in the real world. It was in my role as a landscape gardener and designer that I first realised the usefulness of mathematics in real life, but also how enjoyable it was to do some real-world problem solving.

When I started teaching, I wanted to try wherever possible to have these three elements in my lessons. I wanted to:

- Put the maths into a real-world context;
- Allow students to investigate maths for themselves or as a group; and
- Make my lessons engaging and interesting.

As already mentioned, I wanted to have a real-world context, and in my early days as a teacher, I thought that this in itself would make my lessons engaging. However, this didn't always work out because it was harder than I realised to choose a relevant context that would engage students. Also, some topics just don't lend themselves to any sort of real-world situation!

During my time at teacher training college, I also learned that I wanted to allow students to work on mathematics in an investigational way. I was influenced in this by my tutors, and I had a belief that this learning through investigation was the most effective way to learn. When I say working in an investigational manner, I don't mean maths investigations like those that were set for maths coursework. By investigating, I mean exploring a mathematical situation and learning through enquiry and experimenting.

When I was able to develop a lesson that was rooted in the real world and I was able to facilitate an investigational approach, the third element of engagement normally followed.

It was hard to develop lessons that encompassed all three of my preferred teaching approaches. However, I kept trying to develop lessons using these three elements.

One lesson that kept evolving and eventually met the three elements very well was a lesson on compound interest.

My starting scenario was a story about watching my football team Manchester United at Old Trafford in the early 1980s. I would show a short video of a football match played in 1983 and ask for differences and similarities to a football match today. I would talk about standing in the Stretford End and paying £2.50 for a ticket in 1983, this would normally engage most of the class in a discussion. They would say things like. "I'm a Stoke fan", "Tickets are much more than that now", or even "I hate football". It didn't really matter at this point what they said, I was just pleased that they were saying something and were therefore engaged.

Once I had baited them, I then moved it into some mathematics. I would ask if anyone knew the price of a ticket now? Someone would be able to come up with a reasonable answer to this question.

Let's say we were in 2016 when ticket prices were up to £45. I would ask what students thought about the price of a ticket going up to £45 from £2.50. Responses were varied. Some students thought it sounded better to have been a fan in the 1980s than in 2016, some would say that prices will have gone up since then, perhaps that people weren't paid much in those days. Through this discussion we thought about how we might compare the two ticket prices.

Engaging real-world investigations

We would look at average hourly wages for the two periods and compare the ratio of wage to ticket prices. Often inflation would emerge as being a suitable way to compare. We would estimate what the average price of inflation rate had been over the period. I would find some data that might give us an indication of the average rate of inflation, normally coming out at approximately 3%.

We would then discuss how we might use the inflation rate, normally I would probe and guide them to the idea that if they found 3% each year of the ticket cost, they could calculate the cost of a ticket in 2016 that would be in line with a 3% increase each year from 1983.

Then I would let students have a go at doing this calculation. Responses that I might expect:

1 Finding 3% of £2.50 adding it on and multiplying by 33 years, using simple interest.

$$£2.50 \times \frac{3}{100} = £0.075$$
$$£0.075 \times 33 = £2.47$$
$$£2.50 + £2.47 = £4.97$$

For students doing this method, I would sometimes have to unpick it and help them to realise that they needed to find 3% of the new ticket price each year, and encourage them by saying it wasn't easy but it was a worthwhile endeavour. Starting points varied and some students needed support in finding 3% of £2.50.

2 Finding 3% of £2.50 then adding on 3% each year to the new value, though correct, was very slow, as their calculations might look like this:

$$£2.50 \times \frac{3}{100} = £0.075$$
$$£2.50 + £0.075 = £2.575$$
$$£2.575 \times \frac{3}{100} = £0.07725$$
$$£2.575 + £0.07725 = £2.65225$$

Eventually someone would say "This will take for ever, surely there must be a quicker way?" At this point they were hooked. I could then support them with converting a fraction to a decimal so that they would get £2.50 × 0.03 = £0.075. Then, after further questioning, we would move it on to:

£2.50 × 1.03 = £2.575 followed by £2.575 × 1.03 = £2.65225.

Eventually with careful guidance and questioning, someone would realise that you could do:

£2.50 × 1.03 × 1.03 × 1.03 × 1.03.

I would let them pursue this, eventually they would multiply £2.50 by 1.03 thirty-three times. And then someone would say "There must be a quicker way!"

This process is really time-consuming, but all the time the students are developing an understanding of the maths that they were investigating.

I could at any of the stages have told them what to do next, but that might reduce their involvement and engagement in the task.

When the students were ready, I would ask them if there was a quicker way of writing:

$$1.03 \times 1.03$$
$$1.03 \times 1.03 \times 1.03$$
$$1.03 \times 1.03 \times 1.03 \times 1.03$$

Again, with careful questioning from me, students would see that they could write 1.03 × 1.03 as (1.03)³³, and so on. I would then take my time teasing out that the power or index number in this situation is the number of years.

By the end of this process, we would have the big reveal that £2.50 × (1.03)³³ ≈ £6.63.

Students were amazed that if tickets had gone up by inflation, they would only be £6.63, rather than the actual price of £45.00.

We would then interrogate the formula to identify what the component parts were, I would help them to see that the money value is the 1983 ticket price, that the 1.03 represents 103% and that the index number represents the number of years.

$$T = C\left(1 + \frac{r}{100}\right)^y$$

T = cost of ticket in 2016

C = cost of ticket in 1983

y = number of years

r = rate of inflation

I was always careful to state the formula using the same language that had been used during the investigation.

This opened up more questions, and I tried to encourage them to come up with further questions that could be asked, such as:

- By what percentage did ticket prices actually go up by each year?
- If prices increased by 3% each year, how many years would it take for ticket prices to increase to £45.00?

Students would use trial and improvement by inputting higher yearly percentage increases or changing the number of years dependent on their question.

They might look at other price increases over the years, such as the cost of chocolate bars, a concert, or the price of a house, or a car. The activity was often easily moved to include ratio, or percentage increase and sometimes I got them to plot a graph to show the comparisons.

There were other scenarios that I used that had a useful real-world context. Over time I became better at developing good real-world contexts, I was also influenced by the work of MEI and their contextualisation grid, and by Manchester Metropolitan University (MMU) and Realistic Mathematics Education (RME). Sue Hough from MMU has taught me how to slow down the early stages of working with a context, thus allowing greater engagement with the context.

I have also been influenced by Malcolm Swan's work particularly *Improving learning in mathematics* where I learned how to question better and allow students time to try and investigate the mathematics themselves and how to allow misconceptions to emerge and then work with them. There is a school of thought that you should teach skills and content and then problem solve when students have mastered skills. The "teaching through problem-solving" seen in Japan is at odds with this. But either way, students in FE have been taught how to do something first; so teaching by investigating can be viewed as teaching after they have been taught skills.

Looking at this lesson that I have taught many times with different attainment ranges, it does meet my three preferred approaches of a real-world context, investigating and engaging. But this way of teaching does so much more. It also covers many topics: it included simple and compound interest, percentage of an amount, percentage change, indices, setting up and using formulae, ratio, money, decimal, fractions, approximation, calculator skills, graphs and trial and improvement. Indeed more recently when teaching level 3 Core maths I have developed this lesson further to include spreadsheets!

This type of teaching allows students to make connections across mathematics, contributes to general number sense and helps realise the usefulness of Maths. I have used these types of lessons with students ranging from entry level through to L3, and it should be noted that the mathematics that emerges in the lesson normally matches the level of the students.

Real-world investigational lessons have the bonus of assessing and feedback for both teacher and learner. You must be on your toes and be responsive to learners' needs and be flexible and able to explore and work alongside students. This is exciting though, as you might be investigating with the students responding to a question they have asked, where you too don't know the answer. Lessons like the football ticket prices can be enjoyable for both teacher and student and are, I believe, well worth doing.

Further reading

Realistic Maths Education (RME):
https://rme.org.uk/what-is-rme/about-rme/

The Standards Unit resources Improving learning through mathematics:
https://www.stem.org.uk/elibrary/collection/2933

Teaching mathematics through problem solving:
https://files.eric.ed.gov/fulltext/EJ1089676.pdf

The MEI contextualisation Toolkit:
https://mei.org.uk/resource/9ae5796b-cf76-4ee1-ac9b-08d967d68474/

Why I changed, "From Sage on the Stage to Guide on the Side"[1]

Joan Ashley

Joan successfully taught GCSE Maths resit in an FE college. She has also written and run well-received CPD sessions for mathematics teachers.

Setting the scene

GCSE Maths resit students claim they "can't do maths". They have studied the syllabus at least once and didn't find it that exciting first time round, never mind the second or third time. Many teachers of GCSE resit classes are tempted to rush through the syllabus explaining topics and practising exam questions.

I had "talked the textbook" reasonably successfully for a number of years but I was looking for new, more engaging ways to teach. At a conference I heard about the research of Professor Malcolm Swan, which focussed on learning mathematics through discussion and reflection. This was the stimulus I had been seeking.

Changing how I taught

Trying new ways of working is stressful. I was introduced to new teaching materials and, with colleagues from other colleges, tried them out in the classroom with FE students.

For me, the gain justified the pain. The materials presented thought-provoking situations that often crossed several areas of mathematics in one task. Students were encouraged to work in pairs or small groups, discussing each other's ideas until a consensus emerged. The emphasis was on students gaining a thorough understanding of mathematical situations, rather than arriving at the correct answer as fast as possible.

I was asked to teach a lesson for the first time on the solving of linear equations, in front of six visitors and two video cameras. I was worried about presenting such open-ended materials to the students. Would they reject them? Was the task beyond them? Was I apprehensive – silly question really!

My fears were unfounded. My most challenging students enjoyed this way of working. Differences of opinion were discussed and resolved. Generating questions for each other put students in charge of their own learning. Having to justify their views to each other forced them to think in a way that individual working from a textbook never had. Students who hated algebra, who "couldn't do algebra", who weren't even going to try in some cases, were solving equations with understanding by the end of the lesson.

The activity I used

The activity, with full instructions and recommendations on how to use it, can be found in the STEM e-library.[2]

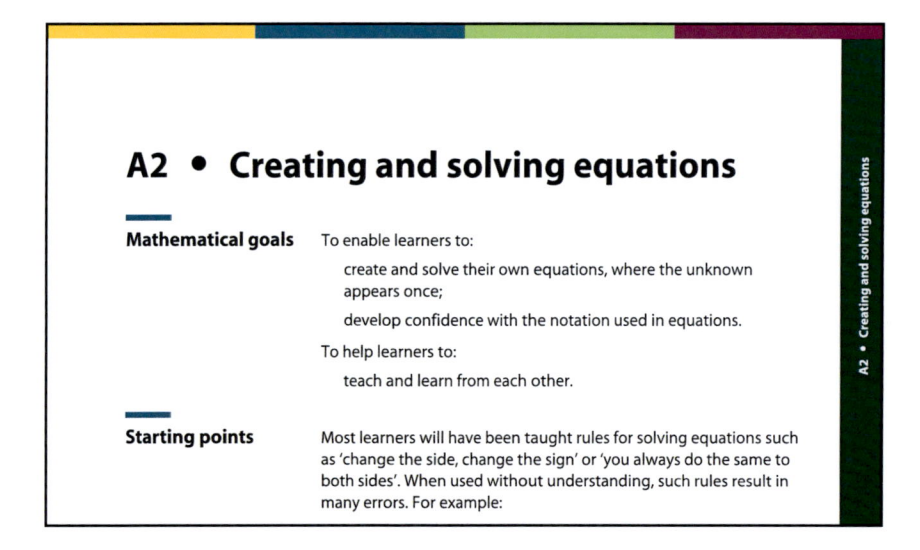

A2 • Creating and solving equations

Mathematical goals   To enable learners to:
  create and solve their own equations, where the unknown appears once;
  develop confidence with the notation used in equations.
To help learners to:
  teach and learn from each other.

Starting points   Most learners will have been taught rules for solving equations such as 'change the side, change the sign' or 'you always do the same to both sides'. When used without understanding, such rules result in many errors. For example:

In summary, students worked in pairs. Each member of the pair created a complex equation from a simple one. Here is an example.

Add 5 → $x = 3$
→ $x + 5 = 8$

Divide by 4 →
→ $\dfrac{x + 5}{4} = 2$

Subtract 1 →
→ $\dfrac{x + 5}{4} - 1 = 1$

Multiply by 3 →
→ $3\left(\dfrac{x + 5}{4} - 1\right) = 3$

Students gave the equation they created to their partner. Their partner undid the equation by reversing the operations, most recent first, as shown below:

$x = 3$

Add 5 / Subtract 5

$x + 5 = 8$

Divide by 4 / Multiply by 4

$\dfrac{x + 5}{4} = 2$

Subtract 1 / Add 1

$\dfrac{x + 5}{4} - 1 = 1$

Multiply by 3 / Divide by 3

$3\left(\dfrac{x + 5}{4}\right) - 1 = 3$

Before the students began to work in pairs, I modelled the activity using student suggestions for numbers and operations. This resulted in some horrendous equations, but it did ensure that everyone understood how to write equations accurately.

The impact on student motivation and achievement

The students were fully engaged in this activity. They even stayed behind after the class to discuss and resolve an error. That was a first! To my delight, they retained their new knowledge and were able to apply it in subsequent lessons, solving even complex equations intuitively. Their negative attitudes had been replaced by a "can do" culture; students were keen to help one another.

This experience confirmed me in my belief that sometimes our expectations of GCSE resit students are too low. At its most basic, algebra is just arithmetic with letters instead of numbers. When experienced actively and logically, everyone who can understand basic arithmetic can understand algebra.

What did I learn as a teacher from this experience?

- My teaching became much less judgemental. I didn't agree or disagree with a student answer but asked for comments, and refused to accept sloppy explanations. This caused no end of annoyance when the initial answer was correct. Students thought that, because I was seeking clarification, their answer must be wrong! Sometimes one student took a deep breath and produced a lucid explanation because they couldn't stand the poor explanations of their peers.
- Sometimes it was helpful to give students a difficult exam question as a motivator, and to work out together what skills they needed in order to answer it.
- I started to ask what students knew about a topic first and built the lesson round that, rather than teaching a rigid, pre-planned lesson. This took more time, but subsequent linked topics took less time than usual because students built on their prior understanding of underpinning concepts and procedures.
- I became more relaxed about "coverage" of the syllabus.
- I tried to make more links between areas of the curriculum.
- I provided practice examples with a range of challenge and invited students to choose their own questions. They appreciated being able to choose which problems to tackle and usually made sensible choices. One student liked to go from the hardest question to the easiest.

What next?

Having discovered that this way of working was effective, I wanted to use more activities of this type, where students could learn together without a lot of teacher direction. Writing such activities takes an enormous amount of time and thought, so I was pleased to find that the *Improving learning in mathematics* box, also known as the Standards Unit box, contained 35 fully tested session plans for GCSE resit maths. You can find these session plans in the STEM e-library[3]. The session plans use the following types of activity.

1. Odd one out

In the triplets below, how can you justify each of (a), (b), (c) as the odd one out?

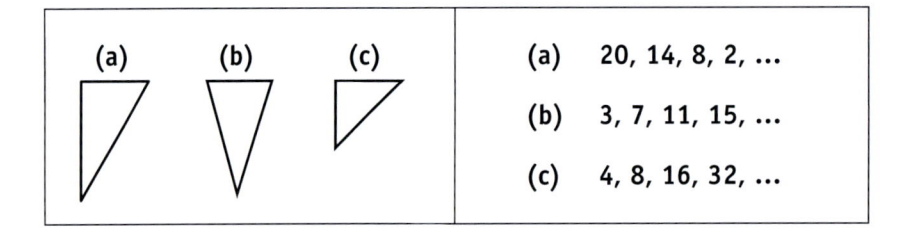

(a) ◸ (b) ▽ (c) ◹	(a) 20, 14, 8, 2, ...
	(b) 3, 7, 11, 15, ...
	(c) 4, 8, 16, 32, ...

Why I changed, from 'Sage on the Stage' to 'Guide on the Side'

2. Interpreting multiple representations

These cards focus learners' attention on a specific aspect of algebraic notation. Learners are expected to interpret each representation and match them together if they have an equivalent meaning.

Your task is to create a different set of cards that will encourage learners to interpret some other representations in mathematics.

These may include words, algebraic symbols, pictures, graphs, tables, geometric shapes, etc.

Try to create cards that require learners to distinguish between representations that they often confuse (such as $(3n)^2$ and $3n^2$ in the example).

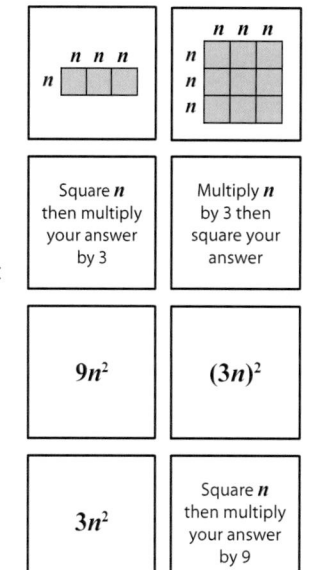

n n n [rectangle] n	n n n [3×3 grid] n n n
Square n then multiply your answer by 3	Multiply n by 3 then square your answer
$9n^2$	$(3n)^2$
$3n^2$	Square n then multiply your answer by 9

3. Classify each statement as always, sometimes or never true

Perimeter and Area

When you cut a piece off a shape, you reduce its area and perimeter	If a square and a rectangle have the same perimeter, the square has the smaller area

4. Using an exam question creatively

Cath wants to hire a car for a weekend.
She obtains the following information from two hire companies.

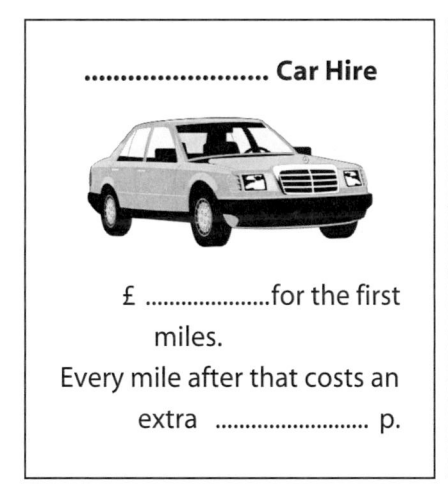

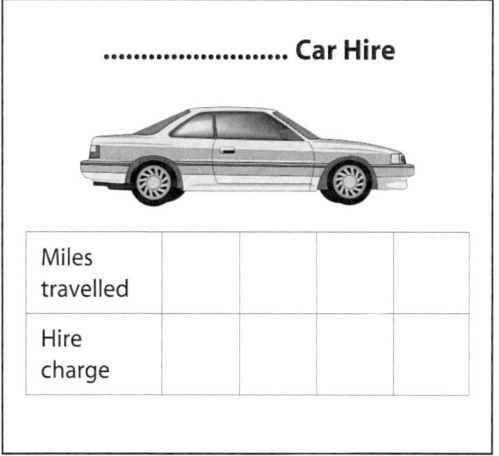

.... Car Hire

£ .... for the first .... miles.
Every mile after that costs an extra .... p.

.... Car Hire

Miles travelled				
Hire charge				

....
....
....

©2024 ATM   45

5. Creating and solving problems

Doing: the problem poser ...	Undoing: the problem solver ...
Creates an equation step-by-step, starting with a value for x and 'doing the same to both sides'	Solves the resulting equation
Draws a rectangle and calculates its area and perimeter	Tries to draw a rectangle with the given area and perimeter

In conclusion

Over the years, like many teachers, I have dipped into this bank of activities, finding through trial and error which ones worked best for my students. Some teachers have modified the activities while remaining true to their design principles e.g. using bar models or ratio tables.

So what would my advice be to teachers who are new to this way of working? I would say "go for it", in your own time and in your own way. The materials are a resource and not a recipe, so don't be afraid to use them in a way that suits you. Have a look at the session plans and try a couple of simple activities with your students first, to see how they respond, and practise not interfering too much (not easy!). Once you have a good relationship with the students and feel a bit more confident, take a risk and try a more complex activity.

This approach refreshes mathematics for both teacher and student. It encourages curiosity and genuine learning by discovery. If you are an experienced teacher, you will already have come across this resource. If you are new to mathematics teaching, do have a look at it. These activities make mathematics learning enjoyable for everyone. Try them!

---

1 – *From Sage on the Stage to Guide on the Side.* Alison King, College of Education at California State University in San Marcos, USA, 1993

2 – https://www.stem.org.uk/resources/elibrary/resource/26953/creating-and-solving-equations-a2

3 – https://www.stem.org.uk/resources/collection/2938/teaching-activities-and-materials

Mean, median, mode and range – a Standards Unit activity

George Lane

George has taught maths at Entry level, GCSE and A level in FE for 14 years. He has a BSc (Hons) in Mechanical Engineering and a PGCE in secondary maths. He particularly enjoyed using the Standards Unit materials with adult students in evening classes.

Improving learning in mathematics

"The Standards Unit: Improving Learning in Mathematics resources ... use active learning approaches originally designed for post-16 mathematics. The resources, and the work of the Standards Unit with leading maths experts in the country, were part of the Department for Education and Skills' response to the Smith Report and offer practical and effective ways to improve learning in mathematics.

"The resources were developed from the work of Susan Wall, a Gatsby fellow working at Wilberforce College, Hull and Dr Malcolm Swan from Nottingham University. The underlying principles to Malcolm's and Susan's approaches are identical, and built on research evidence of the last 30-40 years, which suggests that learning mathematics is far more successful if learners are actively engaged, encouraged to think mathematically and to see links and connections. They also accord with the findings of the Inspectorate, in relation to good practice."[1]

Mainly Statistics S4: Understanding mean, median, mode and range

I have taught this unit in an FE college over many years and have found that it really engages students, particularly adult students such as those studying for their nursing degrees, and it makes them understand what the different averages really mean.

S4 • Understanding mean, median, mode and range

Mathematical goals   To help learners to:
- understand the terms: mean, median, mode, range;
- explore the relationships between these measures and their relationship to the shape of a distribution.

Starting points   Most learners will have met the terms mean, median, mode and range but they may not have a clear understanding of their meaning and the relationships between them. One purpose of this session is to expose and discuss any misconceptions.

I set students to work on the activity in pairs so that they could help each other. Naturally some pairs worked faster than others, but with some teacher input, and, pairs of students helping each other, all were able to work through the unit in manageable chunks. Occasionally I would stop and explain something if I felt it was necessary.

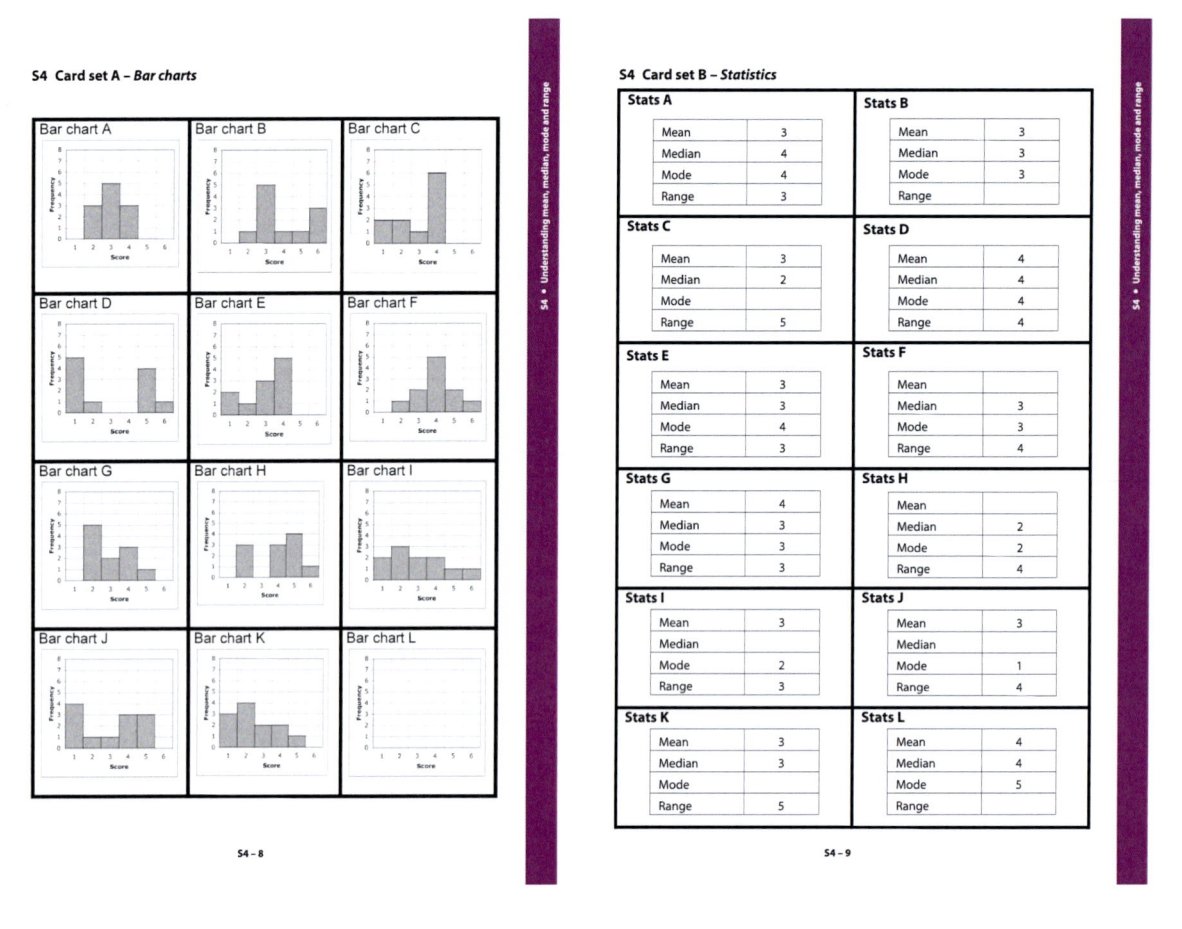

Mean, median, mode and range – a Standards Unit activity

S4 Card set A – Bar charts

Bar chart A	Bar chart B	Bar chart C
Bar chart D	Bar chart E	Bar chart F
Bar chart G	Bar chart H	Bar chart I
Bar chart J	Bar chart K	Bar chart L

S4 Card set B – Statistics

Stats A		Stats B	
Mean	3	Mean	3
Median	4	Median	3
Mode	4	Mode	3
Range	3	Range	

Stats C		Stats D	
Mean	3	Mean	4
Median	2	Median	4
Mode		Mode	4
Range	5	Range	4

Stats E		Stats F	
Mean	3	Mean	
Median	3	Median	3
Mode	4	Mode	3
Range	3	Range	4

Stats G		Stats H	
Mean	4	Mean	
Median	3	Median	2
Mode	3	Mode	2
Range	3	Range	4

Stats I		Stats J	
Mean	3	Mean	3
Median		Median	
Mode	2	Mode	1
Range	3	Range	4

Stats K		Stats L	
Mean	3	Mean	4
Median	3	Median	4
Mode		Mode	5
Range	5	Range	

The cards (and the session plan) can be downloaded from the STEM e-library.[2]

Instructions for this activity from *Improving learning in mathematics*:

Working in groups

Give Card set A – Bar charts and Card set B – Statistics to each pair of learners.

Ask learners to work together, trying to match pairs of cards. They will notice that some of the Statistics cards have gaps on them and one of the Bar charts cards is blank. Learners should try to work out what these blanks should be.

As they work on this task, encourage learners to take turns at explaining how they know that particular cards match.

Allow learners a period of time to get to know the cards, and to think of a good approach to the problem. Learners who struggle with the task may be helped by some strategic hints:

- Try sorting the two sets of cards into order first – from smallest to highest range.
- Now repeat this using the modal values . . .
- Now the medians . . .

If learners continue to struggle, encourage them to write out the raw scores from the bar chart and then sort and organise them in order to calculate the statistics.

During the discussion, the following questions may promote deeper thinking:

- Which two Bar chart cards show a sample size of 12? (J and K).
- Can we tell how big the sample size is from the statistics? (No)
- How do we work out the median when there is no middle number?
  (This occurs on Bar chart J, where the median is 3.5).

This worked for me!

Mean, median, mode and range – a Standards Unit activity

It may be worth stopping the session at some point to discuss these issues with the whole group.

I found that the main area of confusion was between the height of the bar chart and the connection with the frequency since the data was numerical. It was necessary to carefully monitor students' work so that they didn't spend too long down the wrong track.

I kept the results of each of the groups of students and each class usually came up with a new solution for the blank cards. This final element of the unit appeared to be quite daunting to many students when the class was in the early stages of the activity but by the end of the lesson most students were willing to have a go at trying to create a bar chart and it was a good way of stretching most if not all students. Although most of the class would be entered for Foundation GCSE, some students would want to enter the Higher tier paper in order to obtain the higher grades.

I was pleased when one year in the Foundation tier examination there was a question that appeared to be based on this particular activity from *Improving learning in mathematics*. My students were better prepared for this and similar exam questions as they had thought more deeply about how data could be presented and compared.

---

1 – *https://www.stem.org.uk/elibrary/collection/2933*

2 – *https://www.stem.org.uk/resources/elibrary/resource/26992/understanding-mean-median-mode-and-range-s4*

Three sessions that worked for me

Andrew Davies

After graduation, Andrew spent six years in industry before moving into education. Andrew has taught in the secure estate and in FE colleges. He is a Chartered Mathematics teacher and a Fellow of the Institute of Mathematics (FIMA).

Session 1: Tell me about it!

One challenge in FE, is that students, when joining a resit GCSE group, or an adult GCSE group, arrive with different prior knowledge and with different previous experiences of mathematics.

This diagnostic activity is a way of getting a feel as to where students are starting from (level wise), their prior knowledge and areas which will need to be addressed during the year.

I start by writing a number on the smartboard or whiteboard and asking the students to write down three facts about that number. I do not give guidance as to what I am expecting. For example, I might write 15 in the middle of the board.

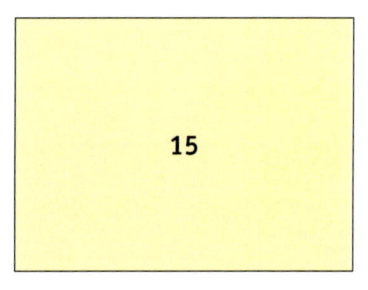

15

After giving the students five minutes to write their three facts down, I collect the ideas from the students, one fact at a time, and write them on the board around the original number. If someone gives an answer, which is that it is a bus number or the age of someone, I still write it down.

I make it clear to the students that they should not panic if all their answers have come up earlier and they have no new facts. I also tell them that if anything is mentioned or talked about that they didn't know before or have forgotten, they should make a note of it.

If a student uses a mathematical term, it is important to ask a secondary question to check their understanding. For example, if the number is 15 and someone answers that 15 has the factors 5 and 3, I ask questions such as:

- Are there any other factors?
- Can anyone explain what a factor is?
- Is there something else which could be called the opposite of a factor?

If a student said, for example, that 15 was a whole number, I then ask:

- Do you know a mathematical word for a "whole number"?
- Can you tell me other numbers that are also integers?
- Can anyone tell me, the mathematical words for other types of number?

Three sessions that worked for me

My board part way through the session:

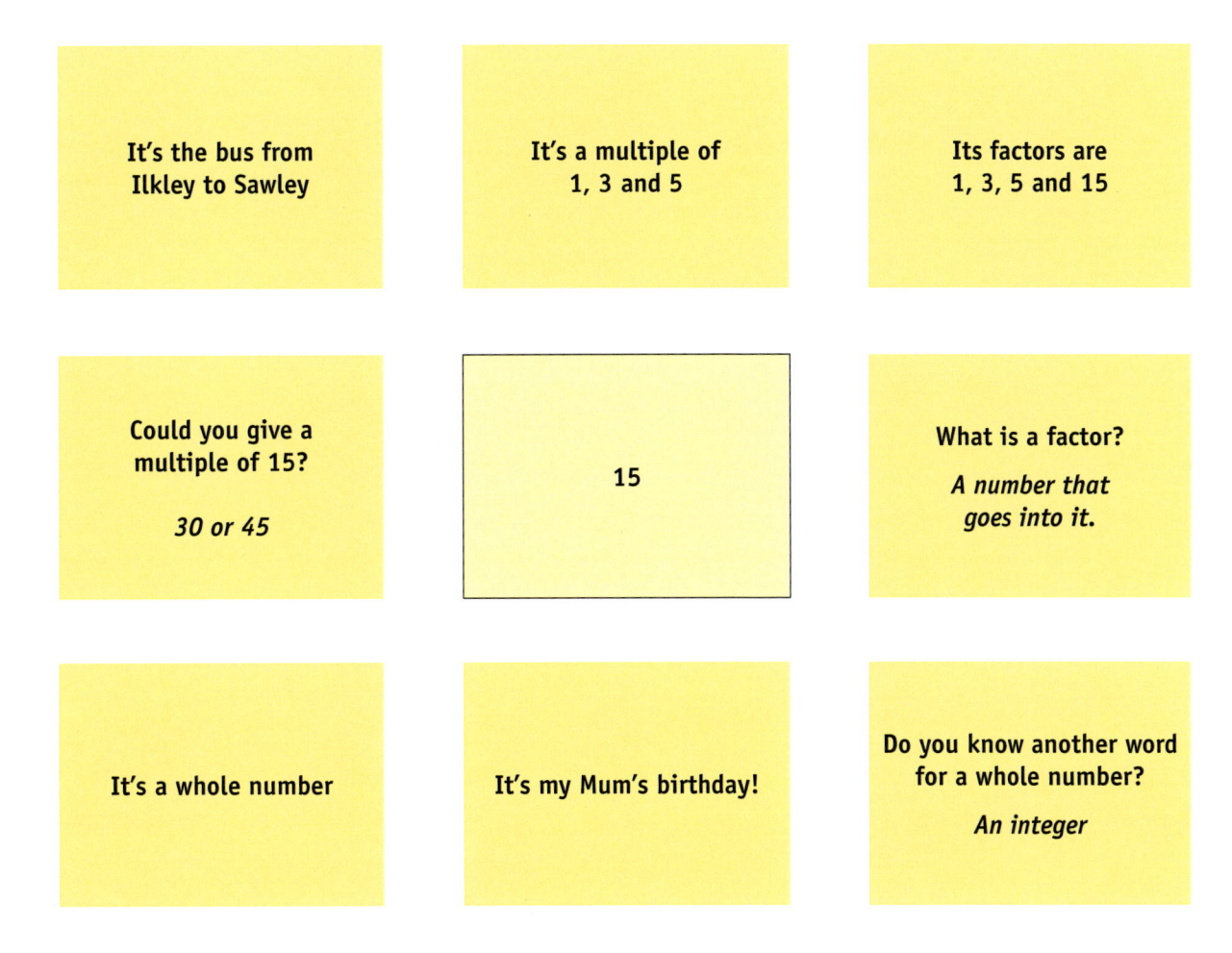

It's the bus from Ilkley to Sawley	It's a multiple of 1, 3 and 5	Its factors are 1, 3, 5 and 15
Could you give a multiple of 15? 30 or 45	15	What is a factor? A number that goes into it.
It's a whole number	It's my Mum's birthday!	Do you know another word for a whole number? An integer

Once I have collected all the students' facts about the first number, I repeat the process with another number (possibly a prime or square number this time). While I am collecting facts about a prime number, I plan to ask questions such as these:

- How do you know it is a prime number?
- Can you give me another prime?
- Is 1 a prime number?

Towards the end of the session, I go over what they have shown me that they know. For example:

- You know what a factor is.
- You know what a multiple is.
- You know what a prime number is.
- You can give examples of prime numbers.

If you use mini whiteboards, you can get the students to write their answers on the mini whiteboards and hold them up and you can then write the list from what you see and ask supplementary questions from them. One advantage of this method is that you can add other facts that none of the class has written down, but which you want to talk about! For example, if none of the students have included a fraction fact or a percentage fact, you can add those to the list on the board.

©2024 ATM   51

You are not restricted to numbers when you are doing this activity but could use shapes or ratios or sequences of numbers etc.

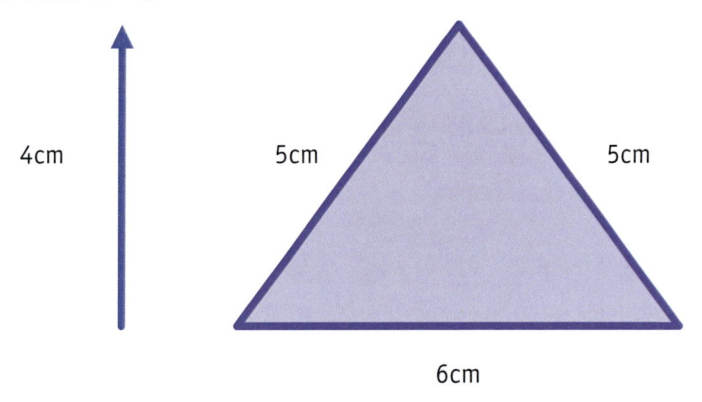

[Triangle with sides 5cm, 5cm, base 6cm, and height 4cm indicated]

Some additional questions that I would ask about the above diagram could include:

- Could you draw another triangle with a perimeter of 16cm?
- What other types of triangles are there?
- Can someone come and draw an equilateral triangle?
- Can someone draw a right-angled triangle?
- Can someone draw a right-angled triangle that looks different from the one just drawn?
- Can someone draw a right-angled triangle that looks different from the previous two? And so on.

It is surprising how much you can learn about the students through this activity. It can:

- Give an understanding of the level of their knowledge;
- Show what areas need reinforcing;
- Reflect what they are already comfortable with;
- Give the students an opportunity to build confidence;
- Remind students of previous knowledge; and
- Reveal topics/knowledge which has not been covered in the past.

Session 2: Arithmetic progressions (or arithmetic sequences)

Before starting this session, I make sure that all students are able to calculate the terms of an arithmetic progression, preferably by substituting numbers into the formula:

$a_n = a_1 + (n - 1)d$ where a_n is the nth term, a_1 is the first term, n is the number of terms in the progression/sequence and d is the common difference.

The students will each need paper, pen and a calculator. If possible, I give each student a small individual whiteboard and a marker to use instead of paper and pen. You will need a set of cards (Set A) with two numbers on each card: 1 and 30, 2 and 29, 3 and 28 and so on to 15 and 16 and a second set of cards (Set B) with the numbers 15 to 30 on them.

The aim of the session is to ensure that students can calculate terms in an arithmetic progression and that they are also able to calculate the sum of a specified number of terms in an arithmetic progression. The activity can be extended to generating the formula for the sum of the first n terms.

I start by asking the students to write down the first five terms of any arithmetic progression on their whiteboard (or paper) and ask them to hold up their whiteboards (or paper).

Now I ask at least three students to explain why their progression is an arithmetic progression. If any student has a progression with a negative difference, I ask that student to explain why their progression is also an arithmetic progression.

I tell the students to check the whiteboards of all the students sitting near them or at the same table. Are all the numbers correct? If not, can they explain to each other why they aren't?

I then ask the students to write down the formula for a progression on their whiteboard and get them to hold them up. After this I go through these steps:

1. I write the first 4 terms of an arithmetic progression on the board, for example, 3, 7, 11, 15.
2. I divide the students into pairs and get each student to pick one of the cards from Set A (the cards with two numbers on them) and ask them to calculate those two terms in the arithmetic progression on the board. For example, if they pick 6 and 25, they calculate the 6th term and the 25th term.
3. I tell them to add their two answers together and compare their answer with their partner.
4. I ask each pair to write their answer on a whiteboard and get them to hold the answer up.
5. I then ask, "Is it a coincidence that all answers are the same?"
6. I ask, "Why are all the answers the same?"

I repeat the process for a second arithmetic progression and again write the first 4 terms on the board, for example, 100, 94, 88, 82 ... and then repeat steps 2 to 6 above.

Then I ask:

- How could we use this to find the total of the first 30 terms?

If they don't know the answer then I ask:

- How many pairs were there? ($\frac{30}{2}$)
- What would happen if there were 20 numbers in the progression?

I make sure that they make note of the result $S = n/2 \, (a + L)$ where S is the sum of the terms, n is the number of terms in the progression, a is the first term and L is the last term.

Finally, I ask each student to select a card from the Set B cards (the cards numbered 15 to 30) and calculate the sum of the initial progression they were working with, up to that term.

If I feel any student(s) needs to go deeper I ask the question "What if you had picked a card with n on it?". Towards the end of the session I get that student or students to explain what they have found out to the others in the class.

Session 3: Graph investigations for students sitting the Higher paper

This session can be split over two sessions and can give the opportunity for further work between sessions. Before this, in a previous session the students had drawn graphs by hand from a table of results.

My aim in this lesson is to give students the opportunity to practise graph drawing, become familiar with graphing software and become able to recognise the effects of changing different coefficients and constants within equations upon their graphs. The session(s) also give students the opportunity to practise investigation techniques and write a report of their findings.

For this session the students need graph paper and access to a graph drawing software (e.g. Desmos or Autograph) or a graphical calculator. Sometimes I ask the students to work in pairs.

I start with the group together and ask the students to draw $y = 3x + 2$ and then investigate what happens when the coefficient in front of the x changes? I insist that they draw three graphs by hand on graph paper and then if they wish to, they can continue using the graph drawing tool. While they are doing this, I will ask pairs or the whole group questions such as:

- What happens when the coefficient is negative?
- What happens when the constant changes?
- What would the line $y = 2x + 4$ look like?
- What would the line $y = 5 - 2x$ look like?
- Where would it cross the y axis?
- What would the gradient be?

At appropriate moments, I ask a pair to come to the board and draw a graph on the board.

I then get the whole class to draw on graph paper $y = 2x^2 + 3x - 3$.

Again, I ask them to investigate what happens when the coefficients or the constant change. I allow them to choose whether to do this on graph paper or by using the software program. If using the software, I suggest that they use a separate screen for each coefficient that is, a screen for the coefficient, a screen for the x^2 coefficient and a screen for the changing of the constant.

I also ask questions such as:

- What happens if the x^2 coefficient is a fraction/decimal?
- What happens if the x^2 coefficient is negative?
- What happens if the coefficient of x is a fraction/decimal?
- What happens if the coefficient of x is negative?

I tell the students to note down what they find and then test what they have found on a quadratic of their own.

If any pair finishes, I ask them to consider cubic curves:

- Without drawing could they forecast what they would expect when they change the constant?
- Is that correct? Test it.
- What happens when you vary the different coefficients?
- What happens if there is no x^2?
- What happens if there is no x?

Again I expect them to note what they have found and to test their findings on another cubic.

These three sessions have worked for me and my students many times.

Creating GCSE Maths revision cards
Bernadette Evans

Bernadette has been teaching maths to adults since 1999 - as well as other related roles such as delivering training, writing quizzes and creating video content for Functional Skills maths. When teaching, Bernadette likes to hand matters over to the learners so they can take responsibility for their learning, support each other and occasionally expose those very useful misconceptions.

Overview

Previously, I had asked the learners to create revision posters in small groups and then to do a presentation to the whole group. Although this worked well, there was an emphasis on presentation skills and many learners were nervous about the delivery. I wanted to use a similar activity without the presentation aspect.

The following is an activity where the learners design and create revision cards. By designing the cards, they are in fact revising the topics they need to focus on. Writing questions and explanations using their own preferred methods are both skills that involve a high level of use.

1 Learners familiarise themselves with revision cards

Each learner was given a different revision card from a published set. The revision cards were double sided. On the front they had a topic heading, a brief explanation, and a multiple-choice question. On the reverse they had the answer, the working out to this answer with added explanations, a tip (for example a non-calculator method), things to watch out for (common errors) and a final top tip. The class individually spent time looking over a card and using it to answer similar questions from the textbook.

2 Learners list the aspects of the cards they liked the best and what they would include in their cards

Learners paired up and discussed what it was about the cards that they found useful. There then followed a whole group feedback, and common themes were pulled out to decide on a design. I sketched these on the board for the front and the back of the cards. Examples included the cards being divided up into boxes, the use of different colours for different parts of the card, such as examples, questions, answers and hints or tips. The learners also wanted to use similar language for each section e.g. "If you only remember one thing …." for the final tip at the bottom of the back of the cards. It was decided that there would be four cards per A4 sheet, and then size of text and how much information was to be on each one were also decided.

3 The tutor creates a short list of topics and allocates pairs of learners to each topic

I had decided in advance which learners needed to revise particular topics based on prior work and assessments. Putting the learners into pairs, I gave them a topic and asked them to create four revision cards for it. I also asked them to think about what kind of questions they struggled with within that topic. They used their notes and exercises to narrow the topic down to four particular skills and style of question.

4 Learners design draft copies of the cards for the tutor to check

Each pair of learners took responsibility for two cards each, regularly conferring and supporting each other. When they were happy with their designs, they swapped the cards within their pair for peer review. I provided a list of things they needed to check including grammar and spelling, correct questions and answers and overall presentation. Finally, each pair handed their four draft copy cards to me for checking.

5 Learners create the revision cards and submit to the tutor for production

Having checked the cards and provided feedback, I returned the draft copies to the learners who corrected any mistakes, made improvements if required, and showed me these corrected versions for final approval. They then created the cards. Depending on available facilities and the skills of the group, this can be done electronically or by hand, and both have their advantages.

However, I found that handwriting the cards meant less time was spent on getting to grips with the Equation function of Microsoft Word. In addition, since they would be completing exam papers by hand, this was better preparation. I did need to curtail the time spent by some learners embellishing the cards to make them look attractive by reminding them of the card style agreed in step 2. I then printed the cards onto card, one set per learner. (The cards could also be laminated.)

6 Learners use the revision cards

In the next session, the learners used the cards for support in answering exam questions on the topics I had selected before step 3.

7 Conclusion

The most useful part of the whole activity was the writing of explanations in their own words and making their explanations concise enough to fit on a small card. In addition, the writing of questions was challenging, and some learners needed to be steered away from reproducing questions they found in the textbook or online. However, I did allow for a certain amount of replication as long as the figures were different. The overall success of the activity depended on the careful choice of topic and its allocation to the learners who were most in need of developing skills in that area.

This worked for me!
For teachers of students resitting GCSE Maths

Edited and compiled by Fiona Allan

Published February 2024

Association of Teachers of Mathematics

2A Vernon Street

Vernon House

Derby DE1 1FR

Tel: 01332 977891

©2024 Association of Teachers of Mathematics

Some diagrams are reproduced from the Standard Unit's *Improving learning in mathematics*.

https://www.nationalarchives.gov.uk/doc/open-government-licence/version/3/

Copyright
The whole of this book is subject to copyright and permission is granted for these pages to be reproduced for use in the purchasing institution only.

All rights reserved

Printed in England

ISBN 978-1-912185-37-5

Further copies of this book may be purchased from the above address

www.atm.org.uk